LEFT
in the
GARDEN

Adrienne

Be blessed

Robin Diana Faldheitolett

LEFT
in the
GARDEN

PIERRE F. D'HAITI, III

To order additional copies of this book, contact:

Xlibris
844-714-8691
www.Xlibris.com
Orders@Xlibris.com
812975

Send all correspondence to the address below, attention: *Left in the Garden*
Pier III LTD
PO Box 55483
Bridgeport, CT 06610

Matthew 13:37–43 New International Version (NIV)

[37] *He answered, "The one who sowed the good seed is the Son of Man.* [38] *The field is the world, and the good seed stands for the people of the kingdom. The weeds are the people of the evil one,*

[39] *and the enemy who sows them is the devil. The harvest is the end of the age, and the harvesters are angels."*

[40] *As the weeds are pulled up and burned in the fire, so it will be at the end of the age.*

[41] *The Son of Man will send out his angels, and they will weed out of his kingdom everything that causes sin and all who do evil.*

[42] *They will throw them into the blazing furnace, where there will be weeping and gnashing of teeth.*

[43] *Then the righteous will shine like the sun in the kingdom of their Father. Whoever has ears, let them hear.*

In loving memory of my deceased parents.

They were both devoted parents and committed to their cause. We honor you, and your children celebrate your life and all your accomplishments.

Pierre Joseph d'Haiti
1936 Sidurant Limbé Accul – du – Nord;
1970 Port–au–Prince, Haiti.

Marie Josée Boussiquot Bien-Aime d'Haiti Midi.
Sunrise, October 6, 1942, Ridoré La Valle de Jacmel.
Sunset, May 8, 2020, Bridgeport, Connecticut.

To the youth and young adults of this world reacting negatively as the result of confusion, hurt, disgust, and disillusionment, who are perhaps searching for the missing link in their lives or possibly facing emptiness.

To women with breast cancer, men with undiagnosed mental illness, individual dealing with suicidal thoughts, depressed and the lonely person, this book is a reminder that you are not alone.

To couples in a dysfunctional marriage, the person on the edge of causing major disaster to self or others, may this book inspire you to look for your purpose in life as an alternative to destructive behaviors.

To you who may be in a garden that is full of despair, there is hope.

CONTENTS

FOREWORD

I feel honored and privileged to congratulate Pastor Pierre F. D'Haiti of Faith Community Church of God on his book *Left in the Garden*, which shares the story of his life from childhood to adulthood.

Pierre has positively impacted the Bridgeport community and beyond through his early work in Connecticut with the Haitian Coalition for Advancement (KAPAB). He started the KAPAB movement to mobilize Haitians in Connecticut to become US citizens and also as voters. As a result, thousands of Haitians in Connecticut have become registered voters. I also applaud the work he has done with Haiti Works, Inc. He mobilized the transportation of a fire truck to Petion-Ville, a sister city in Haiti that was adopted by our great city of Bridgeport. He has served our city of Bridgeport well in his previous role as a planning and zoning commissioner. In addition, he has served on many boards and committees.

Pastor D'Haiti has done a fine job educating the community with his publication of the *African American Yellow Pages*, the *Caribbean-American Yellow Book*, and *Association des Pasteurs Evangeliques Haitiens de CT (APEHC) Newsletter*. In addition, he has co-authored *Haiti-Smile & Life*. His commitment to Haitian cultural awareness is evident by his dedication to host the yearly Haitian Heritage Month Flag-Raising and celebration during the month of May in collaboration with the Mayor's Office of the City of Bridgeport.

Again, congratulations on your book, Pastor Pierre F. d'Haiti on the extraordinary journey that led you the destiny of *Left in the Garden*.

Joseph P. Ganim, Mayor
City of Bridgeport

NOTE

Flowers and plants in a garden, or in any other environment, are designed by nature to adapt to time and seasonal changes. We too must adjust according to events, times, and seasons in our lives. As such, *Left in the Garden* speaks of subliminal messages I've discovered and uncovered throughout my life. I call these messages or experiences Instructors.

One must understand what subliminal messages are: "existing or functioning below the threshold of consciousness intense enough to influence the mental processes of the behavior of an individual." Thus, the conscious mind is awake and aware of what is going on in its surroundings. The unconscious mind is not awake and not aware of what is going on. The subconscious mind, which is the threshold of our mind, houses our emotions, thoughts, ideas, feelings, fears, griefs, hurts, pains, sufferings, doubts and desires, including our history.

The best way to understand subliminal messages is by looking at the top of an iceberg, overlooking a calm freezing lake during the winter months; as beautiful and small as it may seem from a distance, below is a huge piece that controls the seen object. It is the same way with our subconscious mind which stores our memories, our history, and our experiences; that is where anger, bitterness, and resentment find their roots.

For those of you who are suffering and seeking help but cannot seem to find hope, it is no coincidence that this book was placed in your precious hands because it was written with you in mind. My prayer for you is that you will let God handle all your problems. "[6] Be humble in the presence of God's mighty power, and he will honor you when the time comes. [7] God cares for you, so turn all your worries over to him." 1 Peter 5:6-7 (CEV)

Rev. Pierre Fils d'Haiti, III

SPECIAL THANKS

Thank you to my wife Sherly B. d'Haiti for growing with me as we travel through the desert, down the rough valley, up the rocky mountain, and through the fluctuating seasons of time.

To my children David, Abigail, and Olivia, your love for me continues unabated. Thank you for allowing me the time away from you to work on this project.

To my siblings Mike, Ralph, and Martine, thank you for your confidence, affection, and constant support.

My three children:

David Sedar d'Haiti, Abigail M. d'Haiti, Olivia S. d'Haiti

My siblings:

Pierre Junior and his wife Marie d'Haiti
Gladys d'Haiti and her husband Gueslin Charles
Michel Lifet and his wife Magalie Buissereth d'Haiti
Ralph and his wife Charis Williams d'Haiti
Marie Martine d'Haiti and her husband Wilfrid Bristhole
Kevin Midi

To my nephews:

Reginald, Bryan, Aaron Crossland, Daniel Ryan d'Haiti; Marcwin Bristhole, and Guesly Charles

To my nieces:

Emanuela Charles, Najusca Charles, Anseline Charles, Widnard Bristhole, Jolia Bristhole, and Brianna d'Haiti

PREFACE

I count myself fortunate during my lifetime to have encountered many people who influenced me during my journey, whether close relatives, friends, or even acquaintances. They have passed on wisdom they amassed over the course of their lifetime. While this book is largely the result of that, it is also my effort to draw the different threads given to me and knit them together in my own way. Personal perspective and outcomes all depend on how one views the challenges that present themselves and what one does with them. I name the challenges Instructors because through what they have brought to my life, I have learned so much. I desire to share these lessons with you.

FIRST INSTRUCTOR - DETERMINATION

My parents were hard workers. The family on my father's side was from the northern part of Haiti, in a village called Sidurant Limbé in the Accul-du-Nord. My grandfather was Ajuan d'Haiti. My grandmother was Amici Bony—we call her Mann Na. Together, they had six children: Anne Marie d'Haiti Silencieux (Manteo), Antoine d'Haiti, Andre d'Haiti, Edmé d'Haiti Fluery, Rose Isna d'Haiti Filidor, and Pierre Joseph d'Haiti.

My maternal grandmother's real name is Gelise Boursiquot, and she preferred to be called Mante Liz by her grandchildren. She had one child, Marie Josée. She was born in the southern part of the county, in a village called Ridoré la Valleé de Jacmel. She moved to Port-au-Prince at a young age in search of a different life. She was determined to have success in her endeavors. She opened a grocery store in Petion-ville. My mother's father, Theodore Bien-Aimee (Papa Dò), was from Leogane, a township outside of Port-au-Prince. He was an architectural designer and construction developer. He had thirty-five children, and my mother, who was conceived outside of his marriage, was child number 14.

SECOND INSTRUCTOR - FAMILY UNITY

My father cherished family togetherness. He loved staying in touch with his siblings and relatives. My father was a handsome, dark-skinned fellow and a talented auto mechanic technician. The type of work he did ensured that his hands and his clothing were dirty at all times. That came with the territory. Most people from the northern part of the country had dark skin; in my father's case, he was no different, and in addition, he worked on cars that made him appear darker. There was a little preferential treatment given to young men with lighter skin color, particularly by Papa Dò when they came at the gate to talk to my mother. My father greatly desired my mother, so he pressed on 'til he won Papa Dò's heart.

My mother had a different skin color—folks from the southern part of the country have light skin and are called mulattoes. Her father, Theodore Bien-aime, or Papa Dò, was an architectural designer and construction developer and had thirty-five children—Marie Josée was child number 14. Papa Dò believed in family unity. Therefore, his children were not left off with their mothers; he brought them home with him. He built his house a certain way to support his children under one roof. He did this because his wife was not able to have children, so the consensus was to bring the children home. I am not sure whether all the women really wanted to give up their children to him, but he believed that his children should be with him. He had rules that governed his household—one being that his children, though from different mothers, were to live with him, and they were to become doctors, lawyers, officers, nurses, engineers, or architects.

Before he passed, he was blessed to see a police officer, a doctor, a nurse, architects, and engineers—all the professions he had dreamed of, and that was a blessing. Papa Dò believed that a family that lives under one roof should eat together, laugh together, cry together, and be unified. Yes, it was difficult for my father to be with my mother because of the rules that Papa Dò set up; yet another challenge was my mother's elder brother who was like a security guard, helping Papa Dò keep watch on the girls. Nevertheless, love prevailed between my father and mother.

THIRD INSTRUCTOR - SUCCESS

Pierre Joseph d'Haiti graduated top of his class from École Professionnelle JB Damiere, a well-known technical school in Port-au-Prince. He specialized in diesel mechanics and worked on gas-operated motors; he favored the Ford Motors. He had a dream one day of opening a mechanics shop, and that he did. It did not take him too long to open a second shop. He became very successful; he had many clients, including the heads of ministries. His shops were in charge of servicing their private vehicles.

My father had two other children from a previous relationship. He had a boy named Pierre Junior—we call him Pierrot—and a daughter named Gladys. I am very fond of them.

FOURTH INSTRUCTOR - COMPASSION

We had one large mango tree in our front yard. One day during mango season when I was about two years old, and Papa asked me to come to him, saying, "Come to me, my son."

I stood next to my dad and asked Papa to get a mango from the tree. I pointed to it. "That mango way up there, Papa."

He noticed it and threw a stone at it. He missed it, hitting the wrong one. I started crying. He did what a loving father would do to calm a crying child. He said, "I will try it again." He threw another stone, and this time the stone hit a branch, bounced back, and hit me on the left side of my forehead.

I started bleeding. He rushed me to the general hospital to have the cut sewed up. I had four stitches. Then he brought me back home to nurse me. He would not let anyone come near me. Not even the maid could touch me. A visible memory of my father is the scar on the side of my forehead and the way he held and consoled me in the hospital while the doctor was fixing the wound. What I learned from my father was love for people, including children, persistence, compassion, and giving. At the end of the week after payroll, he would go to the nearby neighborhood and give to the poor. He was a loving father, attentive to his children and his wife.

FIFTH INSTRUCTOR - THINGS CHANGE

My mother, Marie Jo, as she preferred to be called, was on the introverted side. She loved flowers, gardening, and reading poems, especially *Les Fables de la Fountain*. I learned a lot from her about how to handle suffering. She was a woman of great faith. As a young wife settled in Petion-ville Delmas, she had lost her husband in the early years of her marriage. She was young and had to face life raising three boys when she had just given birth to my little sister. She quickly learned to be a widow when my father was found brutally murdered in 1970 behind the cathedral in Port-au-Prince, a Roman Catholic church located one half mile from Papa's mechanic shop in Post Marchand. Today, standing in that exact location of the shop is the Church of God of Post Marchand. The morning after, my father's driver showed up by the house and asked my mother for his boss. She told him that he did not come home the previous night. He said to her, "Come with me," and he drove her to the morgue in Port-au-Prince to identify her husband's body. What do you do when things change? In her case, life had never been the same since.

SIXTH INSTRUCTOR - PERSEVERANCE

My mother always sang this song, "Si jodi a mwen vivan se gras an ou segne." If I am alive today, Lord, it is by your Grace.

The atrocity she endured at the hands of her in-laws was unbearable. She often had tears when the memories of the past came across her mind. She often said how blessed she was to own her house. She could come and go as she pleased. What she was referring to was the fact that when she turned on the lights, she was rebuked. Even when she flushed the toilet, she was yelled at. Life in Evanston was bad.

She persevered through it all, even in her desert. She had no relatives, no friends, and did not speak any English. She had to fend for her life in a strange world.

SEVENTH INSTRUCTOR - PERSISTENCE

There are none other quite like my siblings; my brothers Mike and Ralph and my sister Martine were particularly important during my formation. They taught me about tenacity, and that lesson has aided me in different aspects of my life. My father's other children from the previous relationship were kept in Limbé, so we did not share the same upbringing, and our relationship with them was different.

We were kept secluded from the outside world after my father's death. We were fenced in and not allowed to go play with the neighborhood kids. We had a decent-sized yard with all kinds of trees and vegetation. We had no male model to look up to.

I loved to debate. I was always saying and doing things to seek attention, often getting into trouble. I was a hyperactive kid, creative, and a good hunter. I loved to take mechanical items apart and research them. I enjoyed hunting birds and lizards (*zandolit* and *mabouya*). I made my own sling shots. Yeah! I was a sharpshooter. I could catch a bird and/or lizard from any distance.

The vocation that chose me had to do with loving and caring for God's children. I am the pastor in the family.

My elder brother Mike was into cars. He enjoyed carving and making cars out of tin cans. Some of the car designs he created as a child, I now see on the street! He was ahead of his time. Unfortunately, he had not been given the right exposure. If he had, I am sure that one of the vehicles on the road today could have been made by my brother. Mike was certainly good at what he did; he was exceptionally talented. He picked up my father's trade, and he is a master mechanic today.

My twin brother Ralph was into creating houses out of mud and pebbles. He designed beautiful structures and was very good at his craft. Some of the structures he built were up-to-date. Well, today he is a successful architecture designer.

My little sister, Ma, as we call her, embodied motherhood. She is still a nurturer—kind and sensitive. She cares for people. Well, guess what profession she chose? She is a registered nurse!

In all our professions and/or vocations, I found persistence was a key component because we each kept at it until we obtained results.

EIGHTH INSTRUCTOR - FRIENDSHIP

There were people I met along the way who helped shape my perspective of life. They always reminded me that everything would be okay. These include people like Nicolas Jean Guillaume (Papi) and his sister Onide (Manmi). I befriended the family, and they accepted me as one of their own kids. Only one man could call me Pedro-ti pierre for short. He had earned my respect, and I could be real with him. And Manmi, God bless her soul, always had a prayer for me and thought one day I would do something to change lives. Well, Manmi, God answered your prayers.

Through their friendship, I learned about who my father was—the type of man he was. Yet in various ways, I was still searching for my father. There is something about a person's biological father that makes a difference in their life as a child and even as an adult. There is a vacuum—an empty spot that can only be filled by a father. I believe in the African metaphor "It takes a village to raise a child." If it were not for that village, where would a young black male such as myself be? In these United States, I could have gone in a different direction; I could have been self-destructive or sought attention from unhealthy sources. What would I have become?

NINTH INSTRUCTOR - HUMBLE BEGINNING

When we arrived in America—Stamford, Connecticut, to be exact—we lived on Fairfield Avenue on the west side, across the Fairfield Commons Projects. Later on, the family moved to the Merrell Avenue Projects. Around the corner, two blocks away, there was a lot of drugs and gang activity, but we survived, maybe because we were focusing on the better life that America offered.

Building number 42 was a bit calmer than the other buildings. Like the saying goes, one may come from the ghetto, but the ghetto is not the person. We saw our home as a blessing. We learned not to let the environment define who we were. We held this view in order to get to our desired objectives. We had to work hard. We were always busy working and going to school, focusing on our goals. Shortly, thereafter, we (my brothers and my mother) raised enough money to move the family to a beautiful house in a nice residential neighborhood in Norwalk, Connecticut.

We survived the west side neighborhood. I am grateful for that experience of having to share an apartment with three rooms—a kitchen, a living room, and one bedroom—with eight other people. My brothers and I shared a large closet room. We slept like sardines, and the entrance to the bathroom was through our room. We had no privacy. At the Norwalk house, we had become the family my mother had always dreamed of.

TENTH INSTRUCTOR - GOD

The greatest instructor that ever existed is God Almighty, the omnipotent, omnipresent, omniscient God. I say the greatest because at the point of destruction, he showed up, and he brought GRACE. Growing up feeling less-than, with no father figure, the only way to get attention was to do something ridiculous. Nonetheless, he brought LOVE. At the age of six years old, I was beaten and received the worst treatment (which was very much deserved for what I did). I was spit on and ready to be put in jail, with keys thrown away, but he had MERCY. At that point, people were right about me; I was a dangerous kid with a criminal mind. His GOODNESS changed my path.

ELEVENTH INSTRUCTOR - EMPTINESS

Internal emptiness can cause any good person to behave irrationally. It can affect how we react toward one another in relationships, whether in the marriage, work, social settings, and even in how one performs in the bedroom.

I paid a price one day for burning someone's backyard, along with their stuff. But God has a way of showing up in time of trouble. God sent an angel to rescue me, a six-year-old boy, who was being treated like a true criminal and getting ready to be thrown in jail.

Most children will go through a desert experience at some time in his or her lifetime and will never understand what the root cause of the desolation is. "A *root cause* is an initiating *cause* of either a condition or a causal chain that leads to an outcome or effect of interest" (WK). The way a person behaves—whether depressed, spiteful, mischievous, lonely, vengeful, resentful, or vicious—may have to do with their upbringing—the untold story of why certain things happen. Those behaviors are often a sign—a cry for help. When attention is not given, it is easy to notice these signs.

Sometimes a young person has a desire to have a tête-à-tête, a private conversation between two people. They do not want to have a conversation that is one-way. They want to be able to open up to someone who will not become aggressively loud or condemning to the point it causes them to become angry or destructive. Sometimes parents or guardians must bear the responsibility for the cause of that condition because of their lack of patience and good communication skills.

When a person seeking help does not find it at home in their parents, the most profound people in their lives, it makes sense to them to look for other sources of support. So that person sometimes turns to clubs or groups, such as gangs or prostitution rings, and ends up engaging in detrimental, undesirable acts. All the while the only thing the person was searching for was attention and a little conversation.

TWELFTH INSTRUCTOR - NO MATTER WHAT

What I learned from this instructor is that no matter what, one must stay the course and remain focused. Life may throw you a curve ball; if and how you catch it will determine your course of action. It is only based on how you perceive it. The vicissitudes of life will distract you to a point of introducing depression and discouragement, but your ability to see the future in a positive light depends on your ability to remain focused. Through that process, you will be inspired to pursue your interests and dreams, no matter what life throws at you.

The enemy of our souls will enter the scene to destroy you. He cannot do anything else but disturb, confuse, and eventually eradicate you. "The thief comes only to steal and kill and destroy" (John 10:10). To steal what? Our dream. Kill what? Our hope. Destroy what? Our future. In the very same scripture, Jesus said, "I have come so that you may have life and have it more abundantly." You perhaps were born on the wrong side of the tracks, so to speak, or others may say you are from a mediocre family, but that's okay. Wherever you are from—a rich family or a poor family—whatever your status may be—God's plan is to fill your life with goodness.

My siblings and I were constantly reminded as teenagers that we were not going to make it in life. We grew up in America, in a household with a stepdad constantly reminding us that we were nothing. Unless the word of God is full of error, according to *Jeremiah 29:11*, *"For I know the plans I have for you, declares the Lord, plans to prosper you and not to harm you, plans to give you hope and a future."* Thank God that though we grew up in a confused household, dysfunctionality did not define who we were.

CHAPTER 1

What is A Garden?

*Thanks to one of the Homiletic Heroes, Dr. Myles Monroe,
for his brilliant book* God's Big Idea, *from which I borrowed
this passage to draw a point on the subject of garden.*

A small parcel of ground used to grow vegetables, fruits, herbs, or flowers.

Gardens are marvelous things. It is amazing how even a little plot of carefully cultivated fruit trees, vegetable plants, or brightly colored flowers can totally transform an otherwise drab and ordinary landscape. More than almost anything else on earth, a well-cared-for garden signals the presence of life in its fullest abundance, vitality, and beauty. There is something about a garden that stirs an inner chord in the spirit of most of us, a chord of peace, harmony, and rightness, as if to say, "this is the way nature is supposed to be." And of course, that is true.

What does your garden look like? Is it dry, despairing, hopeless, or desolate? When you examine your current situation, what makes you feel confused? Could it be that somewhere in your life, you were disappointed by someone whom you loved? Could it be someone who told you that you will never be anything? That can cause you to feel stuck in the moment, where your inner being is angered by what happened or what was said because you did not expect it from that person. Could it be your father, who walked away from your family when you were young, avoiding family responsibilities and causing you to fend for your life as a child? Peace and harmony will never come your way because there is a missing link—unfinished business—a task that was never completed. Have suicidal attempts knocked at your door when dealing with difficult situations? Remember, "Weeping may endure for a night, but joy comes in the morning" (Psalms 30:5 AMPC).

Every garden needs a gardener, someone to till the soil, sow the seeds, nurture the young plants, and prune, shape, and groom them for maximum fruitfulness and productivity. It must be someone who truly has a heart for the garden, someone who loves it and is completely committed to its growth and success.

Even the Garden of Eden, God's original kingdom outpost on earth, needed a gardener. God did not create the garden and leave it to fend for itself. A gardener was necessary to tend it and nurture it and ensure that it fulfilled all of God's will and desires for it.

God placed Adam and Eve in the garden as its stewards and caretakers, king and queen of the earthly domain. They were gardeners certainly, but neither of them was the master gardener. Until the day they disobeyed God, lost their position, and had to leave, Adam and Eve worked in close concert and harmony with the true master gardener of Eden—the Holy Spirit of God—who, unlike them, had been present and intimately involved in its creation.

Gardens are known by the consistency, quality, and abundance of the fruit they produce, and these are direct reflections of the skills and character of the gardener. According to Jesus,

> [43] *No good tree bears bad fruit, nor does a bad tree bear good fruit.* [44] *Each tree is recognized by its own fruit. People do not pick figs from thorn bushes, or grapes from briers.* [45] *A good man brings good things out of the good stored up in his heart,*

and an evil man brings evil things out of the evil stored up in his heart. For the mouth speaks what the heart is full of. ⁴⁶ Why do you call me, 'Lord, Lord,' and do not do what I say? (Luke 6:43–46 NIV)

The quality of the fruit depends on the nature of the root. Sometimes the evil spirit runs the show.

The writer in Galatians helps us understand this clearly. Galatians 5:16–26 New International Version (NIV)

¹⁶ So I say, walk by the Spirit, and you will not gratify the desires of the flesh. ¹⁷ For the flesh desires what is contrary to the Spirit, and the Spirit what is contrary to the flesh. They are in conflict with each other, so that you are not to do whatever[a] you want. ¹⁸ But if you are led by the Spirit, you are not under the law.

¹⁹ The acts of the flesh are obvious: sexual immorality, impurity, and debauchery; ²⁰ idolatry and witchcraft; hatred, discord, jealousy, fits of rage, selfish ambition, dissensions, factions ²¹ and envy; drunkenness, orgies, and the like. I warn you, as I did before, that those who live like this will not inherit the kingdom of God. ²² But the fruit of the Spirit is love, joy, peace, forbearance, kindness, goodness, faithfulness, ²³ gentleness and self-control. Against such things there is no law. ²⁴ Those who belong to Christ Jesus have crucified the flesh with its passions and desires.

²⁵ Since we live by the Spirit, let us keep in step with the Spirit. ²⁶ Let us not become conceited, provoking, and envying each other.

Every day we all make choices that determine which fruit will manifest in our lives: either the bad fruit of the pretender or the good fruit of the master gardener.

Anyone can be left in a garden; depending on the circumstances in your life, a beautiful garden can turn into a desolate place, a place of emptiness, a position of numbness, a hurtful location, or a depressive environment. The garden can be anything that surrounds you physically or emotionally and that which affects you psychologically.

CHAPTER 2

Babies Talk

What does the house sound like with four toddlers talking and moving nonstop? What was it they were saying? Let us hear:

Ti-Michel = Michael
Mama, didi vav = Mother, Dadi needs the potty
Mama, didi vav poopoo ate ya = Mother, Dadi needs the potty, he had a number two on the floor
Mama, didi pipi = Mother, Dadi urinated
Dadi = Pierre
A ya da da = Somebody is here
ya ya = Hello
e e e e e = I am hungry
a ya da da = Father is here
a ya a ya didi= I need help
oooou didi pipi = Dadi urinated
oooou didi poopoo = Dadi soiled himself
zouzou = Ralph
kite ye epo = Leave it alone
an iye a = over there
ma = Martine
nen nen, zou, di di = Someone is up to something

CHAPTER 3

Toddler Memories

The most memorable moments with my father were during kite season. This baby boy knew how to enjoy his father. Usually, during this season, everyone would show off their talents with the kites. My father created a six-foot-tall kite. We called this size kite grandou. It took quite a few guys to get that thing up. It was a fun time for flying competitions, seeing who could fly their kite the highest and whose kite can go the longest distance or can stay in the air the longest.

In addition to having kite fights that were represented by teams, sometimes the aim of the competition was to see who could outdo the other or who could take who down from the air; it was very interesting stuff. The idea was each would have a kite designed with a razor blade on the tail. As the kites fly in the air, we would attempt to strike the opponent on their line, whereby the blade cuts it and brings the kite down. Now whoever captured the kite from where it landed, whether individual or team, was the winner. Sometimes it seemed an impossible task because the kite was still being moved by the wind, and it could land God knows where.

Well back to the concept of grandou, the huge kite, one day, this eighteen-month-old desired to fly the grandou, and my father said, "Okay, we can get you up there."

He created some type of safety harness and tied me up on the line. Because of the strength of the grandou, along with the wind velocity, the extra weight made it easy to fly the grandou. Once I was strapped in, away I went. I am not sure of the height I reached, but I could see the top of the houses. That was the most fun time ever in my life.

We don't see these types of activities anymore, those that bring parents and kids together. It would be nice to include kite-flying activities in our inner cities' recreation department, whereby parents can bond with their kids.

CHAPTER 4

The Day After

According to eyewitnesses, my father was wounded while he struggled fighting three men. He suffered multiple stab wounds as he was struck with a dagger under the left arm, and he was left bleeding to death in the car. The brutal murder took place the night before he was to travel to America, to Michigan, to work for the Ford Motor company. My father had a simple plan—to prepare the way for his wife and children to come sometime later, but he thought bringing his brothers and sisters to America first was best.

The day after the murder, my father was found dead behind the cathedral in Port-au-Prince. His driver showed up that morning, late from the normal routine, to pick up my father to go to work, but this particular morning, the driver was to bring him to the airport to catch the flight to Chicago, Illinois.

My mother's usual routine, before the sunrise in the dewy morning, was to go in the front garden to pick fresh herbs so the maid could prepare tea for my father before he headed out to work. As was typical, I accompanied her on her early morning trip to the yard. As I walked with her, carrying the little straw basket, I did not have underwear on or a diaper nor shoes. She had on a beautiful light blue see-through satin robe that revealed her contour as the early morning wind blew. She had given birth to my little sister about two and half months prior, and I had turned three years old three months before.

This is the story behind not having any undergarments on, according to my mother: "Daddi did not like to wear undergarments because when he had a number one, he quickly pulled the diaper off, and when he had a number two, he would stop and say, 'Dada, didi, poo poo, Dada, didi, poo poo,' until someone cleaned him." As such, the nickname "Daddi" came about. I was full of joy being with Mother in the garden.

Suddenly, my father's driver showed up rather late. He approached my mother a bit slow and asked her a simple question. "Where is Boss Pierre?"

She replied, "My husband did not come home last night. He was out with some friends."

He said to her, "I need you to come with me to go identify."

She asked, "Identify what? Where?"

He replied with no remorse or emotion, "I think he is dead."

My mother started screaming as if she lost her mind, "Amwayyy, Amwayyy, Amwayyy Pierre!" This means "cry for help" in Creole.

She ran to the house, continuing to scream for help. You can imagine what it was like as people came out their homes responding to her call.

Meanwhile, I was left in the garden with no pants and shoes, not knowing what happened. I started screaming and crying because my mother was screaming and crying. I think I may have dropped a number two on the ground, perhaps because I was scared and alone in the garden. She went inside, put on a different outfit over the pajamas, and took off with the driver.

I was afraid. I was lonely. I was stuck in that position, and it felt as if my whole world left me. It didn't feel right. My little body felt stunned. I was there for quite some time, and no one came to assist me or search for me. I was calling, "Mannnmy, Mannnmy, Mannnmy." No one came out to get me. "Mannnmy," I called.

I'm not sure if I remembered the way back. See, when one is in a state of panic, memories can be blocked. Could it have been that I was so scared and confused that the only safe position for me was to curl up like a ball on the ground? I was groaning because I was in emotional pain. I could not describe the loneliness—the deep pain I felt. I was angered and did not know why they left me. I could not describe the hurt. No one ever asked me if I was okay. I was treated like any typical kid crying for his mother. No one ever comforted me as a little boy. I was basically ignored. Children have feelings too, and they should not be dismissed because of their stature.

While in the garden, I heard the maid calling my name, "Daddi," the nickname my father called me. "Daddi, dah, dah, dah, where are you?" she continued.

As I heard her voice, I began to call out, "Mama—Papa, Mama—Papa."

She came over, grabbed my little hand, and walked me inside. No one asked me where Mama went, and even if they were to ask, I don't think that I would have given a clear response to such a question. Tears continued down my face, as I continued to call out, "Mama . . ." Mind you, the area was not crowded or well developed. There were not too many houses. It was like a field with trees, bushes, and flowers; it was a nice area to live in. By 8:00 a.m., the rest of the neighborhood heard of the situation, and everyone came out wondering what happened. Later the driver came by with some men demanding to see my mother, and the maid told them that she left with someone in a car and left Daddi behind in the garden.

Among the men were my father's apprentices and my father's nephew, as well as a man who lived further up the road in Petionville. He had taken one of my father's trucks and wrote on it, "la terre promise," meaning "the promise land." This man enjoyed chastising us every time we walked by his house, reminding us, "I got it now," referring to the truck. They waited until my mother got back, and when she arrived at the house, they surrounded her as if they were roughing her up and demanding things. I have no idea why they encircled her, but whatever they were doing made her react like a super mad woman.

All I know is her life was never the same. She became delusional and was crying constantly. She became insecure. She was being tormented and harassed for shop keys and cars. She even had a gun pointed at her head. It seemed like they had no sympathy for the loss of her husband; they had no mercy and no compassion. Among the people harassing her were my father's little sister's husband, who had a heated argument with my father regarding his desire to have Papa's little sister in marriage. He was just an apprentice learning the trade and working for my father.

The man was in love with Papa's little sister. He desired her so bad, he was willing to do anything. Papa wanted someone of better quality than this man—one who was not arrogant and vicious. So during their heated conversation, my father said these words, and Mama heard, "Over my dead body you will marry my sister!" My father stuttered, so in conversation, it would always sound as if he were fighting.

Well, not even a week after, my father was buried. This man convinced my aunt to marry him. Some said he had her trapped in witchcraft magic. Mind you, this is the sister Papa adored, and this is the sister who was Papa's confidante and best friend. You know, in a family, there is always a sibling who is favored over the others—well, she was the one. After his death, all Papa's auto mechanic tools were somehow in this man's possession, and he was able to have them shipped to Evanston, Illinois.

Upon our arrival to America, we went to visit my aunt in Evanston. There was this man bragging about my father's mechanic tools; of course, he's an auto mechanic technician now. He admitted that he possessed them not for memory sake, but because he earned them. No one dared to ask how he acquired them; after all, we were kids, still grieving the death of our father. He also mentioned other men in Haiti, as well as my father's relatives, who had other things like cars and trucks. He said, "We are not saints and not perfect. I was not the only one involved. There were other people, including close relatives, who participated in his demise."

In 1981, since the first time we met him, and since my father's death, he has had the audacity, in a laughing manner, to say that he knew who killed ti-Pierre (that is what Papa's friends called him). This man was very confident talking about what happened. "It was well planned." It seemed like my aunt was trapped in a hole with this man because of what Papa had told him about not having her as his wife. As such, he made her life, as well as my brother Pierre's life, difficult. It all made sense—every time my mother saw my father's picture, she would burst out crying until she revealed the reasons.

CHAPTER 5

Where is Hope?

Between 1970 and 1973, my mother was faced with a lot of challenges, including humiliation and threats from my father's former employees, vendors, and even from his apprentice. As she greatly struggled to raise four kids, my little sister, Martine, who was born three months before my father was murdered, was sent to live with Aunt Lilianne in Port-au-Prince. The boys stayed with Mante Lise, Lilianne's sister. Later, in 1975, Marie Jo fled to America in search of a better life for her family. Unfortunately, she ended up in Chicago at the house of those who plotted to have her husband killed. I guess the necessities of life will cause anyone to end up at the mercies of even one's enemy. She was mistreated by in-laws much worse than by my father's former apprentice, who defied my father who did not want him to even have a date with his little sister, much less marry her.

Marie Jo always quoted this Haitian metaphor, "femen nen w, bouwe dlo sal la," meaning, "close your nose, hold your breath, and drink the dirty water." It was later that Marie Jo began to explain what the dirty water was. It was an expression to encourage one who is going through hardship to hang in there and fight their way out. This man was very much involved in the plot, and he bragged about it. He was very rude and aggressive toward my mother. This man changed the lock on the door to the house. Marie Jo was locked out in the snow, in the freezing cold weather in Evanston, Illinois, the suburb of Chicago. What Marie Jo thought America would be for her was deceiving, for she saw nothing but hopelessness.

Unfortunately, she was now faced with the real-life situation of living with her enemies. She was constantly chastised when she used the shower, in addition to sexually assaulted by my father's brother in-law. She was not allowed to utilize the house laundry machines; she had to go the distance into town to do her laundry. Walking with a pull cart through these white neighborhoods in the early 70s was a disaster waiting to happen.

Marie Jo was not allowed to use the house telephone to make phone calls. When she wrote letters to her father who was living in Brooklyn, New York, and to her mother in Haiti, she never told them what she was going through. She kept it a secret until she found her way out of the situation.

When my father was alive, Marie Jo had maids to cook and clean for her and even drivers to take her where she desired. She always called herself "Je suis la fille du roi," I am the daughter of the king. I thought she was referring to quotes in the Bible. It wasn't until our conversation and listening to her stories that I picked up what she really meant by that. When my father was alive, she lived like a princess.

The hardships she endured were unbearable to a point where she thought of committing suicide many times. But when she remembered she left her children behind, she had hope one day to reunite with them, so she began to plan her way out of there. Somehow she was able to make a collect call to her father in Brooklyn. Papa Dò asked her to come to live with him in New York. She wrote the address on a little piece of paper. She took a Greyhound bus to New York, and she was free from that place. While in Brooklyn, as the years went by, she began to search for Mante Lise's relatives who lived in Connecticut. Later she moved to Stamford where she remarried, to Maurice Midi.

CHAPTER 6

Without A Father

My father bought a piece of land at the beginning of the suburb of Port-au-Prince, Delmas, in the border of Petion-ville the Lindor Cartier in (Jakay) across Musseau neighborhood. At that time, the area was incredibly beautiful, with trees and various greenery. The neighborhood was made up of mostly middle-class entrepreneurs. All the families in the area had their businesses operating in the capital, including my father. Many of his customers were affluent people from Petion-Ville, so it made sense to move part of his business near the suburb. My father was "a young, good-looking, outgoing entrepreneur—a people person," according to Marie Jo, his wife. So he began a family around the time Francois Duvalier, Papa Doc, was the president. My father had his first mechanic shop business in Post Marchand. The cathedral is about half of a mile away from the shop in a busy area near the popular neighborhood Lakou Mouzin.

I have always wondered what it would be like to be in a house where there is a father figure who is present and active in a young life. I always questioned, what is it like for a teenager to have a man to call dad? What is it like for a girl to know she has a father? How does a young lady feel the day of her wedding not having her father give her away in marriage? What does it feel like to have a father in one's life? I also questioned how one's behavior would be affected if they had the voice of a dad to guide them and give them direction when faced with various issues or decisions.

Not having a dad is a difficult thing. It makes you think, who can I bounce ideas off? Who can I have a man-to-man conversation with? Who can I look up to? Who can give me directions? Who can be that strong voice I need to hear that will lead me to change my course of action? When I obtained a good grade in school, or was playing sports, like soccer (my favorite), I did not have a father who would say, "My son, job well done."

I wish I had a dad to stand on the sidelines to cheer me on when I scored a goal, or when as a goalkeeper, I made a nice catch. When I had a victory, who was there to celebrate with me? My friends had their fathers to show them how to ride a bicycle; who did I have? My friends' dads showed them how to drive; who did I have? As a young adult and body-building champ, I did not have a father to share my victory with or to show me off when I won.

Many of our young men and women are growing up with fathers in the home, but it's as if they are not there because though the body is there, the connection is missing. The dad could be in the home physically, but emotionally, he is absent. I can empathize as I grew up in a home where the male figure had no strength and no emotional attachment. As a result, I had to search for fatherly attention in other places. How was it for you? What led you to seek that attention elsewhere? Was it the physical abuse? Was it the sexual abuse? Was it the verbal abuse? What effect did the abuse have on you as a child, an adolescent, or perhaps an adult in a dysfunctional marriage situation?

The negative effect of this missing link on a child will likely be issues with future relationships because as humans we become fragile and inaccessible because of the isolation that has mounted so high without checkup. Many of our children's negative behaviors, such as temper tantrums, hyperactivity, even quietness, or other attention-seeking behaviors, could be from lack of the father's physical or emotional involvement in the child's life. Any male can have a child, but it takes a man to be a father.

Sometimes children will do things to get attention because they are feeling neglected in some way. As parents, we tend to be blind to the reasons a child acts out, ignoring the needs behind the attention-seeking behavior. The child may be given a timeout or a medical quick fix (drugs) to induce the child's behavior.

Though we didn't have a strong father figure in the home, we had Grandma Mante Lise. She moved in to support us after my mother left the country to America. I will say this: if it were not for the strength of Mante Lise, I do not know where we would be; she was our guide and our protector.

CHAPTER 7

What Did it Look Like Without A Father?

When it came to her grandchildren, she was a different person. She was like an eagle during the day, watching over her grandkids; and she was like a cherub at the night, keeping watch over us. She slept with one eye open, and she did not go to bed unless all her kids were accounted for. She made sure every night that she prayed with us and made sure we recited our prayers. She fed us and made sure that we were always clean. We never had to beg for anything. When going to church on Saturday, she usually carried a twig in her hand. If we made any wrong move on the street, she lined us up, and we got a switch. We need grandmothers like that today, who, no matter where they are, whether in the home, or in public, discipline their grandchildren.

There was hatred and lots of jealousy from the neighbors. We were the most hated kids because we were well-maintained. We were not allowed to associate with kids outside of our gate. As such, there were those who hated my father and also wanted to destroy us. Mante Lise understood that very well, and that is the reason she sheltered us and became our shield of protection. Oh yes, there were many attacks on us. Folks set up voodoo traps outside our gate. One time someone placed a booby trap or voodoo trap outside the gate, and my brother Mike went outside and kicked the basket with the calabash ball (kwi) away. His leg was left hanging in the air with his knee bent. He had to be rushed to the hospital. The man who did this testified forty years later that he has been trying to kill us, just like our father was murdered.

After meeting with this man face to face, I confronted him. "What have we done to you that you wanted nothing but the worst for us?" I've come to understand why we were in seclusion behind walls and not allowed to interact with others; my father had enemies—family members, friends, and neighbors.

It was quite scary when one day a man showed up with one of father's favorite cars. Obviously, he stole it. He walked up to my mother, ordering her at gunpoint, demanding the keys to all the vehicles. She went inside and handed them over, and he told her to hand over all the jewelry. That moment was a life-and-death situation. He got what he demanded and left. For the rest of the time that we stayed in Haiti, every time this man would see us, he would terrorize us until my grandmother threatened him. He was the man in Petion-ville who was always chastising us.

Many of the characteristics I inherited are from my father. Even though he did not see me grow up, his spirit lives in me. I know if my father were alive, he would have tried his best to make sure he was actively involved in my life. I see it in the way I operate as a dad to my three children. I find joy in interacting with them and in them interacting with one another. I am involved in every aspect of their lives—sports activities, including teaching them the ropes in sports, cooking, and outdoor activities, including survival skills. I am their role model. The person I am today is not my father's doing; it is not because of his instruction but the presence of God in my life.

I want to leave my imprint on my children, so they know they are my kids; they know they have security and are protected. I want to make sure that my children do not miss any part of me. I want to give them what I desired as a child.

C H A P T E R   8

In Search of A Father

Growing up was awfully hard and difficult. In order to get anything, I had to do something irritating to get attention. As a result, I got a beating almost once a week. I got beaten for jumping from ten flights of stairs, not expecting to get hurt. I sometimes got into mischief and received a butt-whooping for that too. Sometimes I asked why I was getting a whooping. That, however, was taken as disrespect toward my butt-whooper; in my case, that was usually my grandmother. She did the job either with her fist or a twig but never a sandal, which is customary for Haitians to discipline a child. I was never told what I did to deserve the beatings.

The Haitian way of punishing a child is quite different from the American way of disciplining a child. The punishment includes going in the corner on the knees on the cement floor for thirty minutes or so, depending on the incident; sometimes going for one hour or more. One punishment was so severe that I was put in a corner with a coconut metal grater for one hour. The coconut grater is that tin metal grating material used to grate coconut, carrot, etc. The little holes in the grater were so painful; even talking about it hurts. That punishment was for throwing stones on top of a house where they were having a voodoo ceremony. The owner of that house found out it was me, and she went and told Gran-ma. Gran-ma used to say, "I would rather you cry than me cry over your dead body in a casket." That still did not make me flinch. I continued doing mischievous acts, all for attention.

One time I went to hide in the middle of that big mango tree in front of the house. I was shooting sling shots at people as they walked by. At one point, people were just afraid to cross or walk in the area because they did not know where the shots where coming from. I was playing sniper games, and as a result, people were getting hurt; again, this was for attention.

During one semester in college, I encountered a sociology professor at Southern Connecticut State University, who was from Africa and had read my biography. He suggested that I go to a voodoo temple on Flatbush Avenue in Brooklyn, New York, to see a *Ougan*, a voodoo priest who could have me talk to my deceased father. As a young college student, I was so happy that I was going to speak to my father. Does this really exist? I do not know, but in the voodoo culture, it is a practice. I was so desperate and needed to fill in that empty space.

One Saturday morning, I took the train to New York on my way to Brooklyn from New Haven, Connecticut. No one know where I was. I found the place and entered. I asked the gentleman at the desk about the location, and he told me that I came to the right place. I began an interview process with him. I was, of course, willing to spend my money as I needed to find out if this was a legitimate business. I told him what I came in for. I was ecstatic to hear what he could do for me. So he took me to the temple, asked me to drop the money on the floor, and had me sit down on a small chair made of straw.

At that point, I was very scared. I had not a clue what he was going to do. During his ritual, I kept repeating under my tongue, *"Angels of the Lord encamp around about me and protect me." Psalms 34:7 (MSG)* Mante Lise made sure we remembered certain verses in the Bible, particularly this one, and she never let us depart from her presence without saying this verse; it sure came in handy.

Suddenly, the man pulled the chair from under me and said, "Do not to come to this place again, I do not serve people like you!" and he threw me outside the temple, onto the street.

I was certainly on the wrong path. My parents did not know where I was, only that I was on the college campus. My roommate at the time did not know I left the campus to go to New York. Anything could have happened. I was fortunate.

Later on, in my early thirties, I had this deep desire to find out who I was with the hope of finding out what happened to my father. This man whom I had befriended came to mind. Perhaps he could help Unfortunately, he was not there. During my search, I realized that the Haitian man who owned the store near Downtown Stamford had inspired me subliminally to enter an institution that could help me find myself through the mastering of the mind. As a result, someone sponsored me as a freemason. I found out that when you understand the "what," in terms of what you are after, it will be easy to articulate your "why," your objective. So it was easy for me to rise through the ranks. Of course, there were some jealous folks who questioned my knowledge of certain things since they thought I couldn't possibly reach the level I did. Perhaps they thought I was too advanced in knowledge.

You know, when God wants you to go and learn certain things, he will let you do just that while preparing the place for you to prosper. The fraternity became tasteless, and I told God that if he was having me go in another direction, it was his duty to burn all items I have acquired—books, symbols, jewelry, aprons, candles, ties, belts, all of it—and eradicate them from my memory. I stayed far away, without any contact. Guess what? God did just that. My membership lasted about three years, before I abandoned the practice.

After that experience, I came to realize that there is no better friend, and no better father, than Jesus. I started going to church in search of God's presence and the Holy Spirit, in hopes that through him, I would be able to find my father and find true friendship. I asked God to show himself if he was real and to express who he really was in my life. While at city hall during one of the late-night planning and zoning commission meetings, I saw a huge figure on the wall talking to me. No one was able to see it but me. The figure gave me a command. I thought I was going coocoo.

I requested permission for a quick recess. I went to the restroom to wash my face and came back to the session. That night, driving back home, I went the wrong direction to my house—not on purpose. I ended up in the area where the figure and the voice directed me. The instruction was this: "There will be a church from the junk yard to be placed in this lot." I ignored the command.

Two years has passed. A pastor from a church near the local junk yard showed up with an unorthodox plan on a piece of paper. We, all commissioners, thought it was preposterous and utterly ridiculous. The rest was history. Just as the figure said, today a mega church structure is located at that exact location. There, I knew God was real.

CHAPTER 9

Protection

During my teenage years, there was a man whom I was fond of because he enjoyed talking and interacting with young people, especially young men. He taught us self-respect and to be appreciative of other people and to love humanity. He taught us to stay away from gang activities and stay clear of trouble. He held us accountable for whatever we did, even our school grades. He applauded us when we received good marks on our report cards. He encouraged us to hold ourselves high and be the best that we can be. He had a military background. He was the first Haitian to own a multiservice music store near Downtown Stamford. His conversation with us was usually about life and how to conduct ourselves in society as young black men. He usually directed us to the right path, and he enjoyed referring to our Haitian roots. He loved philosophy and metaphysics.

One day a man walked in the store during a time he was having a teaching moment with the four of us. They had a strong, heated conversation that drew my attention, and I became very curious. By this time, the other young men walked away, and I stayed behind listening to the conversation. I guess my presence did not interfere with anything they were saying. The conversation went on for a while. As it came to an end, they shook hands like men do. That caught my attention because everything this man had taught us, he modeled in the conversation. At that point, I said to myself, *I want to be like him.*

So the following week, we all met again, and the teaching became a bit more profound. I asked him, "How can we become like you?"

Of course, the other boys did not understand why I was asking such a question. Afterward, he pulled me aside and began to share with me how I could become my own or, in other words, be the master of myself. That raised a huge question for me. I needed a father figure, and he became that to me during the time I spent with him at the store. He knew that my father was murdered because around the time of my father's death, he was in Haiti, and the obituary in the newspaper told the story.

He told me quite a bit about what he heard had happened. We became close. He was a free mason, and he never divulged any secrets but left everything to my own understanding. I was intrigued by what I saw: the masonic symbols he had at the store and on his vehicle license plate and books he was selling, including Bibles. I became humbled and wanted to learn all this guy could teach me regarding these things, but he did not instruct me. He left it for me to find out.

As the summer came to an end, the school season started, and I went away to college. When I came back to town during Christmas break, we did not have a chance to meet. By the time spring break rolled around, I found out that he died. The interesting question that came to mind was, why? Why do good people have to die? He was the type of teacher who would say, "If you don't know the cause, it is up to you to find out." I began to search for answers concerning his death, and I came to the conclusion that he was sick.

In 1998, I was water baptized at the Ephraim Seventh-Day Adventist Church. I joined the Bethel Memorial Deliverance Church, where I learned a whole lot about the work of the Holy Spirit and his mighty power; he is a wonder. My wife and kids were in another church. To keep order and harmony in our marriage, I thought it was fitting to have the family under one roof, so I left and joined Kingdom Life Christian Church.

This was yet another wonderful encounter as I was selected to go on a mission trip to Haiti. The bishop called me to his office to have a tête-à-tête. I remember I told him that I needed to be examined by the Holy Spirit before I made such a decision. So he said, "Let us pray," and we did. I felt a pressing to let him know that I could not go on a mission trip without getting rid of any or all baggage. He questioned what the baggage was. I said, "Bishop, let me tell you about my journey and how I got here. From my last experience in the lodge, I obtained a briefcase that I need to throw away."

He said, "What's in it?"

I replied, "All the stuff I picked up on the journey while searching for my father."

The last thing I remember that I did before putting it away was praying and asking the Holy Spirit to destroy and burn all of it. I developed such a strong belief in the work of the Holy Spirit, so I put the brief case underneath the stairs where no one could have access to it. I asked the Holy Spirit to do his will and prove that he is all-powerful.

I went back to the bishop's office with my wife. This meeting was sacred because we prayed before attempting to open the briefcase which had buttons with codes on it. As I tried to remember the codes, the bishop was very focused while my wife and I were in prayer. I finally entered the right codes, and the briefcase came open, and all the objects in the briefcase were consumed—burned without the briefcase being damaged on the inside or the outside. To the unbeliever, it is impossible for that to happen—for the briefcase to not be damaged but the items inside turned into ashes. That's when I knew that God was real, and the Holy Spirit was, without a doubt, in control of everything.

I was not in trouble with God, for he had a plan for my life. I needed to remove and get rid of anything that would hinder God's presence from working in my life to accomplish his will. I had to sacrifice the flesh so that God could have his way with me, and he did. In order to understand what happened there, you must have some notion that in my quest for the missing link, I visited the wrong places, I knocked on the wrong doors, I entered through the exit, I joined the wrong crowds, all for attention. When I immersed myself deeply in the activities that were of interest to God, things changed. That was the visible manifestation of God's presence and the work of the Holy Spirit in my life.

> *7-15 Are you listening, dear people? I'm getting ready to speak; Israel, I'm about ready to bring you to trial. This is God, your God, speaking to you. I don't find fault with your acts of worship, the frequent burnt sacrifices you offer. But why should I want your blue-ribbon bull, or more and more goats from your herds? Every creature in the forest is mine, the wild animals on all the mountains. I know every mountain bird by name; the scampering field mice are my friends. If I get hungry, do you think I'd tell you? All creation and its bounty are mine. Do you think I feast on venison? or drink draughts of goats' blood? Spread for me a banquet of praise, serve High God a feast of kept promises, and call for help when you're in trouble—I'll help you, and you'll honor me.*

—*Psalm 50:15 The Message (MSG)*

CHAPTER 10

Seek Attention

One beautiful Saturday during the fall season, my rebellious self was in full motion. Just like every Saturday, I gave my grandmother a hard time about going to church. Oh, I forgot to tell you that I was raised as a Seventh-Day Adventist. We attended Eglise Adventiste Bethanie de Petion-Ville, where I learned leadership; I was a pathfinder, and there I met some of the best people I have ever known. As much as Grandma kept us busy with church activities, I still was missing something. I knew what it was, and I knew I would not be finding it in the church. There were times, especially during the summer and the middle of the fall season, that I was always getting into some type of trouble.

After one of the maids, Jocelyne, went home on Friday around midday, we were left with Sefet for the weekend. Jocelyne was younger and able to move faster, and she liked to fight with Mike, and guess what? Ralph is the only one who never caused any problems. On this Saturday, however, I refused to go to church. I took off and jumped over the gate and went outside to the Lindo neighborhood to play ball with the kids.

As usual, Mante Lise sent Sefet after me. We usually argued all the time for the same reason—she would go and look for me, tell where I was, and cause me to get a beating. So I pretended I was playing in the yard. I heard Sefet coming for me, so I jumped over the gate and was out. Before Mante Lise left to go to church, she made sure that Sefet brought me back in the house, and she did. Mante Lise gave me a serious beating with a twig.

Before she left, she put me on my knees and told Sefet to watch me and wait for her to get back from church. I did not really stay on my knees all that time because as soon as Sefet left to go run her errands, I was off my knees doing mischievous things. I was watching her as much as she was watching me. I was upset, but I did not really care if she told on me again and caused me to get another beating.

Both Mante Lise and Sefet liked to do gardening. They had a nice harvest of corn, pumpkins, avocados, beans, and okra. They had vines that run to the trees into the nearby neighbor's backyard. Do you know that after the harvest, the plants dried up? I was on my way back upstairs, and I noticed a box of matches on the stairs. I took it and went about my business. Later on I became very bored, and I started to play with the matches. I took my little game to the garden. I struck a match and threw it into the dry corn to see if it would light up, and after a couple of tries, the corn leaves caught on fire.

I watched the fire travel to the nearby trees and onto the vines in the backyard of the houses behind me. Mind you, around that time, all the *acajou*, Mahogany tree fruits, were dried up, and they fell to the ground. The area was in flames. I took off running and went to hide on top of an acajou tree. I was scared, wondering what I did. The neighbors were looking for the one who did this. They were now counting the number of kids in the area. Some people said they saw Mante Lise leaving for church that morning with Michel and Zouzou. No one could locate Daddi. Suddenly, I was spotted by the worst guy in the area. His backyard was also in flames.

He climbed up and grabbed me by the leg and pulled me down. He did not let go of my leg, and we ended up on the ground together. All treatment I received that day, I deserved; I was slapped, spit on, kicked, and punched. People were very mad! Somebody took me by the back of my pants, yanked me up, and gave me a wedgie. I was practically walking on my toes as they were taking me to the nearby precinct. They were saying, "Put him in jail!"

"He is a vagabond!"

"He is not worth it!"

"Throw away the key!"

All the while they were still mistreating me with the punches and slaps.

Be mindful that this happened during the time when the Duvalier regime was in power. Jean Claude was president, and the Tonton Macoute oversaw some of the police stations. It was clear—I was guilty of the crime. I deserved what they did to me. [The Tonton Macoute (Haitian Creole: *Tonton Makout*) or simply the Macoute was a special operations unit within the Haitian paramilitary force created in 1959 by dictator François "Papa Doc" Duvalier. In 1970, the militia was renamed the *Volontaires de la Sécurité Nationale* (VSN, Volunteers of the National Security). Haitians named this force after the Haitian mythological bogeyman, *Tonton Macoute* ("Uncle Gunnysack"), who kidnaps and punishes unruly children by snaring them in a gunny sack (*macoute*) and carrying them off to be consumed at breakfast. (Wikipedia)]

Even though I was a child, the little rebellious demons were playing in my head. God had to intervene because there was no other hope. Anything could have happened to me. My act warranted me being locked up, with the possibility of being kept there indefinitely. But God knew my destination.

God knew why I was misbehaving so much. I was after one thing and one thing only—a father's attention. This could have cost me my life. God sent an angel, the grand marshal chief of the Macoute of Petion-Ville. His name was Paul Vericain; may God bless him. He was driving up from below Delmas, and on his way, he noticed a crowd on the street, shouting, "Lock him up, throw away the keys!"

This man had power and authority and could have decided the fate of my life. He came out of his jeep. He stood tall and asked what was going on. The sergeant answered, "This little vagabond set the neighbors' backyards on fire, and the people are demanding we lock him up, throw away the key."

My Grandmother was standing across the street, watching as this all unfolded. They would not let her in to speak on my behalf.

There were those crying who, I guess, knew what was going to happen to me. The mothers were watching with tears, and the young boys my age were watching as things were about to turn dark for me. Based on my actions, I didn't deserve mercy. At least that was my mindset at the time; I felt I didn't have value. I believe people had sympathy even though they were angered by what I did, and rightly so, but I did not deserve to be put away at that age.

The grand marshal looked at me. He took his hand and placed it under my chin. By this time, there were no more tears in my eyes, and my face was all dry. I could not cry anymore. I was shaking as he held my chin. He said, "Look up and look at me in the eyes. What is your name?"

I said, "Pierre d'Haiti."

"How old are you?"

"Six."

"What school do you go to?"

I said, "Institution Mix de Saint Joseph Petion-Ville."

He saw a cry for help in my eyes. I simply had no more tears. I wonder if you have ever been in a distressing situation where, suddenly, your tears have stopped. That was my case; my tears had stopped as he held my chin firmly. I urinated on myself. I lost my self-control during the interview and defecated on myself because I felt this was the end of me. I was very scared.

The only thing I could make out of this situation was that this man was an angel sent to my rescue. I say this because there was something about the way he slowly looked around and stared at the officers and the crowd, saying, "If anyone touches this boy, I will roll my jeep over their body." Before he pronounced the follow-up sentence, the crowd had disappeared. "He is only a child."

I am grateful to this man for what he did. I thank God for sending an angel to spare my life. I am so sorry to those I have affected because of my misconduct and negative behaviors. I am sorry for the lost possessions.

CHAPTER 11

Si-Yad

My seventh year of life must have been the most terrible year for me. It was one incident after another as I was yet again seeking attention.

There was an apprentice at a unisex tailor shop in the neighborhood. This man traveled a long distance to work at this shop. I witnessed an argument between a local food merchant and the apprentice regarding him owing her money. He was not willing to pay for what he had consumed. From then on, I started teasing the man as he walked by our gate and on the street. I was calling him some bad names that really upset him.

One day he decided to revendicate and claim respect from me. So he began to run after me, but I was very quick on my feet. The more he was chasing me, the more I felt he was playing, and I continued on calling him names. People were watching and laughing. I was running on the street and crossing in front of cars. I thought it was a show. He was filled with anger. When he finally caught up with me, he grabbed me and punched me with rage, multiple times on my head. What was worse was the *si-yad*, which is what one gives to another when they use their knuckles, pushing on one's head hard, while sliding them across. This burns the head and is extremely painful. People had to get him off me. Frankly, he did not deserve to be shamed in public by me, nor did I deserve to be physically hurt like that in public, or in private for that matter.

Many years later, while on a trip to Haiti, I visited the shop and found out he no longer worked there. He had opened his own shop in a carrefour. I sought him out and finally found where he was. I had to apologize to him for what I did. I apologized for shaming him with my words and told him to not worry about what he did to me physically because that pain was temporary. He forgot what happened.

The need to reach out to him and make amends was so strong; I had to have closure.

CHAPTER 12

Why?

Celebrating my birthday has always been an issue for me. It was a day that I had my guard up and did not trust anyone. The smile was removed from my face. I intentionally stood busy on that day. I consciously removed myself from people and did not engage in conversation. It wasn't until I became an adult that I realized I was doing all that for a reason. I secluded myself on that day as a profound way to protect myself from other people who could potentially physically harm me. I am naturally not bent on making a big to-do on birthdays, but for that day, the one I will tell you of shortly, I am filled with resentment and bitterness. I enjoyed singing birthday songs for others, but I didn't like others doing the same for me. It would have made a difference to me to have a wise and understanding father there on my birthday to celebrate with me and make my birthday special.

One Sunday afternoon, while celebrating my eighth birthday with friends and family, something terrible happened that made me feel I was in a desert of despair. I was at a complete loss, with absence of hope. When I am feeling hopeless, smiling is hard—birthday or not. On that special day, my birthday, I learned not to ever trust anyone, including those who are supposed to care for me. That day my friends from school, along with family, were at the house.

Everybody was having a good time talking and playing. We were on the gallery with my friends, and I wanted to be kind and serve them a snack first. I started to bring in glass bottles of sodas to each of my friends, about five of them. I was laughing, enjoying the moment.

Suddenly, Mante Lize's little sister, Tante Lilianne, showed up. She had an accident that left her crippled and one leg shorter than the other. We had a funny name for her, "zoukou tap," because of the way she walked. But that is beside the point; no one made any comment or pointed to her disability. She was the one caring for my sister in Port-au-Prince. She was single, never married, and had no children.

All of a sudden, she pulled up to my side and did not utter a word. She took me by the ears and started to twist them. It hurt so much that I started to scream. All the while my friends were laughing. The punishment apparently looked very funny, getting my ear twisted like it was about to be ripped off.

She stopped for a minute and walked away. As tears were coming down my face, I felt ashamed. She came back. She said, "Who told you to take the sodas out?"

I said, "Nobody." I explained that it was my birthday and these were my friends. I wanted to serve them. I did not even finish my sentence before she slapped me so hard.

Let me pause here. In our family, boys and men were not allowed to visit the kitchen, much less take anything from it without asking a servant; it is the rule. That was the first thought that came to mind, yet I still do not know for sure why she was attacking me, even 'til this day. She pushed me so hard, and out of respect for my elder, I did not want to respond in defense. She took all the sodas from the kids, including mine.

She walked away and came back with a tin bowl and hit me on the head with it. Mante Lise saw what she did and said to her, "Don't do that! What did he do to deserve you hitting him?"

She pushed Mante Lise. It seemed like she had it out for me; she was determined to hurt me and anyone that was in her way. She was ready to destroy; she had to finish me. She pushed me to a small room and shut the door behind her. She slapped me and then took a broomstick and beat me with it. When she got tired of using the broomstick, she took another tin bowl, denting it on my head. As I was screaming for help, she locked the door behind her. One way out of that small room would have been to jump out of the window. My brothers Mike and Ralph tried their best to get me out of this situation by throwing objects at her through the window to stop her. They even threatened to deal with her when she got out.

I guess the threat intensified the situation because she beat me all the more, yet no one knew why she was beating me. She continued inflicting pain, pinching me hard, with rage. The neighbors tried to stop her to no avail. Mantel Lise tried to intervene, but it made matters worse. Finally, that woman got tired and stopped, thank God! It seemed like she was so frustrated about something—only God knows what—and let everything out on me. Sometimes you may feel like you are in the desert alone, being destroyed by a relative. You may not understand the reason, and it may not be justified, but God knows why.

Every time I think of this incident, I ask God why he let this woman beat me so much to a point where my face was swollen and I had lumps on my head from the hard objects she used to hit me. Even though this was the worst thing she could do to me that day, I still ask God to forgive her for punishing me like that.

Later, when we settled in United States, in Stamford, Connecticut, my mother sent for her to come and stay with us. Her sister was already here in America, and she was alone back home in Haiti. She came and stayed with us. You know what? Forgiveness can be a b—h! How can a person who inflicted so much pain on you come to live in the same house with you? She could not fend for herself. She did not speak English. She had no way of getting to doctor appointments, immigration visits, or anywhere else she may have wanted to go. As a teenager, I had to put the resentment and bitterness behind me. I had to let go of the grudge and see her as a child of God whom the devil used to do his punishing work on me.

I assisted her as much as I could, though my siblings did not help her much as they were still bitter for what she had done to me. Sometimes, in life, one will never know the whys behind strange occurrences. She went to be with the Lord, and she never revealed her purpose for beating me on my birthday with so much anger and rage to the point of having my head swell.

The God in me is the God of forgiveness and compassion. Yes, it hurt. Yes, the pain was unbearable, but the bruises had vanished. Nonetheless, the emotional scars remained. Only God could remedy the pain and bring peace. I may never know why I experienced this terrible moment on my birthday. I do not wish that experience on anyone, especially a child.

Trying to celebrate Father's Day is also painful; not knowing what happened to my father makes it a traumatic day for me. I become isolated, having minimal contact with others. It is the day I feel the most human disconnection because nobody can explain to me why my father is not here. I become sad, though sometimes I pretend to be fine.

This day should not be commercialized because in doing so, we camouflage the essence of a real father. A real father sees himself as accomplished only when his children and wife are protected and happy.

Sadly, a father's presence in the urban household is almost irrelevant because the child is taught indirectly not to respect the male figure. This lack of respect is often learned through the way society treats men or sometimes the way the mother treats the father. As such, the child develops a disrespectful attitude toward the male figure.

In the child's mind, it is okay to disrespect authority, and they may not learn otherwise until they have encounters with the law. In suburban households, the lack of the father's presence is just as dangerous because the child may be told to go to their room as a way of disciplining them, but while in the room, they are doing everything but reflecting on their behavior. They are using the free time to think—sometimes of ways to be disruptive and self-destructive. They may have drugs or alcohol in their rooms, and while in timeout, they may be indulging in these harmful substances. Parents should reconsider how they discipline their child and if that discipline will produce a favorable outcome.

I believe a father's influential presence is so important. It helps a child learn to respect elders and other authority figures. It helps a child have a sense of character. It shapes and molds a child's life, giving the child a model to look up to. When Mante Lise was having a good day and I was misbehaving, I remember she would give me a paper and pencil to write the reason one hundred times. That usually calmed me down and changed my behavior.

CHAPTER 13

Misunderstood Relationship

First off, we must get a feel for what being in a relationship means. Some aspects of relationships are seeing each other regularly and spending more and more time together, dating, and eventually living together in a marriage situation. Another way of relating could be shacking up in a common marriage with no commitment. There are many different ways to define being in a relationship with someone. But once you are in a relationship, the rules remain the same. There are certain characteristics that make a good partner: understanding, shared dreams, camaraderie, supportive, loyalty, honesty, passion, patience, and love. When looking beyond the traditional ideas of being a partner in a relationship, the question in my mind is, what does it really mean to be in a relationship?

Let us take for instance marriage and what it stands for in the context of a union. It is the legally or formally recognized union of two people as partners in a personal relationship (historically, and in some jurisdictions, specifically, a union between a man and a woman). But in some cultures or older traditions, marriage was arranged; one has no time to learn about the other person. A similar type of marriage relationship is also called planned socioeconomic support, where the marriage is arranged based on certain interests to where there is no true attachment between the individuals—only a monetary one.

These types of relationships can be found among the immigrant community. The purpose for such an arrangement may be twofold. The first reason for this marriage would be to allow a partner to gain legal status in the United States. That partner usually pays in advance. In some cases, they may also pay dearly in another way, especially if living together, in the form of unwarranted verbal and/or emotional abuse. It may become worse if the relationship produces a child or if one of the partners has children from a previous relationship. Sometimes there is a lot of baggage carried from the past, and all the consequences of that can cause one to regret the decision to get into such an arrangement. The weight of the remorse involved can make the relationship seem unbearable.

The second reason for being in this type of marriage relationship is to avoid the questions that come with being without a partner. A woman may not want to face the social stigma of not having a man. People just assume you must be a widow. An unmarried woman with children was not an acceptable scenario, particularly within the religious community. It was expected that she finds a man to be a husband and a father to her children.

Being in a relationship means you are fully in with your partner. You can't pick and choose which parts you do and don't like. Along with the good comes the bad, and being a partner means embracing all of someone. Here are some aspects of being in a relationship:

BEING THERE FOR THE PARTNER. In life, we experience ups and downs. When your partner goes through tough times, you can help by offering support and being their strength. Relationships often get stronger during difficult times because it is when you really learn how to be a partner to somebody. Then when you are the one having a hard time, they will be there to offer you the same support.

TEAM PLAYER. Deciding to be in a relationship means choosing to be on your partner's team. And sometimes that means putting their needs before your own. When you are committed to someone, you consider them when making both big and small decisions. In a relationship, you work together and make room in your life for each other. You are not just an "I" anymore. You are a "we."

BE YOURSELF. Even though being in a relationship means you are a "we," you are still encouraged to embrace all the things that make you you. Not only should you be yourself, but you should also be the best version of yourself. In a healthy relationship, your partner will accept you exactly the way you are, even the baggage you carry. They will never try to make you into someone or something you are not.

RESPECTFUL. One of the most crucial characteristics of a good relationship, if not the most, is respect. It is important to approach all aspects of your relationship with respect. This includes being kind, knowing your partner's limits, and not doing something that would knowingly cause them to be depressed all the time. Arguing is inevitable, but you can handle conflict from a place of love.

CHAPTER 14

Not Easy Telling It

After I was ordained as a minister, my mother confided in me she wanted healing as she realized she had to leave her past behind as difficult as it was. She had to face the reality of the decisions she made. She was in tears, crying uncontrollably, and calling out for help. I thought someone had died. When she finally calmed down a little, she regained her composure and began to share with me some of the worst stories of her life. She told me what she had to endure to protect us after my father died. She shared what she had to do to pretend everything was okay in her current marriage relationship.

At one point in our conversation, she said, "It is harder than what you see. It's been difficult." She began to share the story of what happened regarding my father's death. She told me who was involved and what they did to him. She spoke of how they came after her for car keys, the shops, and everything. She began to share stories of what happened when she arrived in Evanston, Illinois. She expressed that if God was not on her side, she would have committed suicide.

When she married her second husband, in order to keep peace in the relationship, she accepted the arrangement to allow him to not contribute toward any bills, whether rent, mortgage, or groceries. Even though she paid for the green card in advance and in full, she stayed with him for all these years. She accepted the unkind words, the betrayal, and every other wrong just to preserve the marriage union. That was part of the price she had to pay.

The most uncomfortable thing to hear was the arrangement regarding him not contributing monetarily and how she agreed with it. Well, according to her, she kept her part of the deal and suffered through. During this marriage, she was always depressed and had self-harming thoughts. Even though she was aware of the extramarital affairs, she kept her peace.

Throughout the duration of the marriage, she had something festering inside her. One time they went to Haiti, and he dropped her in Delmas and left her there. He did not come back until it was time to return to the United States. She knew where he was; he was not with any of his family members but with his mistresses. She kept silent because she believed in marriage—"'til death do us part."

It made sense as to why my mother was working two jobs and on her days off, would go and clean houses. She did this for thirty-five years. She had a crazy debt to pay. I think this was a form of modern-day slavery.

My mother preferred to use public transportation. The only time she would catch a ride from him was to go to the laundromat or supermarket. She did not rely on her husband for transportation because of how he would shame her. She desired to learn how to drive, but he would not help her. He would, however, always brag about how he would help other women learn to drive and obtain their drivers' license.

We appreciated him for giving my mother the green card (for which she paid dearly for). My mother had to petition for us to come to the United States by herself.

God gave us a can-do attitude and the spirit of tenacity. I taught myself how to drive and found a neighbor to take me to the Department of Motor Vehicles (DMV) to take the test. I passed. I remember the Thursday evening I came home with my driver license; I was welcomed with a back-hand slap from my mother. My stepfather was so happy to see my mother receive me like that. My stepfather did not help any of us, so I taught and helped my siblings navigate through the DMV process.

I encourage any single parent, male or female, that before you bring another person into your life and expose your children to someone, pray and ask God to give you clear instructions and discernment because you will encounter difficulties, and the kids may suffer. Not every deal that looks good is sweet; think twice before making this decision.

CHAPTER 15

Be The Best You

As a young boy, I was fascinated with the sport of soccer. I joined the Valencia Soccer Club in Petion-ville. I played the goalie position. The team practiced at Saint Jean Bosco soccer field, playing on the concrete floor. It was like playing indoor soccer. Interesting enough, I was the best player in that position. When I arrived in the United States, I tried track and field and did not have any luck with it, so I quit. I joined the Westhill School Soccer Team and became the captain during my junior year in high school. Our team was enduring a hard time as our coach had to travel to Africa to handle the death of his mother. Our substitute coach felt I was the best player and should lead as the captain. I led the team to the city championship, and we won against Stamford High School. While in college playing pick soccer, I tore a ligament on my right knee. The injury put me out from playing soccer for a year. I ended up losing interest in playing, but I enjoyed coaching young people.

I developed a passion for body-building. I joined the local YMCA and trained extremely hard. I learned and trained with some of the best in the sport, including AAU Champion Carlo Berci and Mr. Universe Renel Janvier. I followed in their footsteps and became the Fairfield County champion. Body-building kept me very focused and determined.

Be the best you. This statement was the basis for the discipline I developed and used to attain any objective I had. During the period of amateur body-building, in 1990, I told myself that I was competing with myself; therefore, I have to be the best me—on the stage, in the gym, with my diet, and with all aspects of my physique. I did not compare myself with other competitors nor even had the mindset that I was competing against them. I was focused on myself and what I was doing to shine, regardless of what others were doing.

Therefore, when I looked in the mirror, whether in the gym or at home, I saw a winner. This was not a conceited attitude but a way of examining myself every day and striving to reach the standard I had given myself. With this mindset, I would always be ahead of my opponents.

There are different reasons why people go to the gym. Some go for toning, losing weight, and/or physical therapy. Then there are those I call gym rats. They go to look, talk, and distract folks who are trying to maintain focus. They make noise with weights, pretending that they are doing something great. In reality, they are a distraction to the sincerely determined.

I noticed in the gym that there were those who were serious about winning. They were the people I gravitated toward. I tried to get wisdom from them because they had a whole lot to offer aside from a nice physique. I saw that they were more focused with their regimens, which included dietary plans, workout schedules, and body resting. I noticed they were very patient. I tried to emulate those strategies in order to win. I went to the gym every day for two hours. I didn't miss a day. My daily planner was filled three months ahead, and I followed it well. I created a system to work on my physique and my mind, and it helped me know exactly where I was. Physically, I did what I was supposed to do, and my body responded to the regimen I developed. I rarely altered the system, and the only time change took place was during on season and off seasons. During the on season, I would prepare for the competition that was six months ahead. This meant the workout would be different; instead of building mass, I focused on shaping my body. I did more repetitions with lighter weights. I ate more vegetables, proteins, potassium, and carbohydrates and drank lots of water.

On off seasons, my diet consisted of lots of red meat, and protein as a way to gain more body mass. The focus in this season was on utilizing heavier weights, decreasing repetitions, performing more sets, and attempting to maximize strength by increasing the weight. My body knew exactly when and what to eat. It took the nutrients it needed and rejected what it did not need. I also was mindful of when I should exercise; I let my body guide me and inform me when enough was enough and when I needed to rest or sleep. I used reading to help my mind stay focused.

The dietary component has to match with the rigorous workout. You have to be conscious of timing and resting because the body will develop its own habit of taking what it needs and getting rid of what it does not because of the system you created.

In 1990, I weighed in at 149.5 lbs., with a body fat count of 3 percent. I was all muscle. I was able to create a symmetrical physique, where calves, thighs, gluteal, latissimus dorsi, deltoids, pectoral, biceps, and triceps were all in proportion.

On the stage were fifteen other contenders. Some used steroids for muscle enhancement, and some developed their bodies in other ways. I chose to remain all natural. I saw Pierre in competition with Pierre. Therefore, I had to be the best me on stage in the group and in the individual performance. As a result of the hard work, dedication, and commitment to being the best me, I won the Fairfield County Championship and the "Best Poser" trophy.

The "best you" mindset encouraged me to remain steadfast in the face of adversity. One such challenge, which I will get into detail about in a later chapter, was when the Big Yellow Book and the SNET Yellow Pages' executives recognized that I was on their radar screen with my companies, Caribbean American Yellow Book and the African American Yellow Pages. As a result, both companies agreed to give me access to the Yellow Pages publisher

Code. I became the first African American to hold the Yellow Pages publisher Code. Yet again, with the "best you" mindset, I gained an audience with the city council of Bridgeport and with a four-star general of the United States Navy from the Southern Command. The general agreed to transport a donated fire truck on the C-17 military transport aircraft from the city of Bridgeport, Connecticut, to Petion-Ville, Haiti, a city adopted by Bridgeport.

FORMULA FOR THE BEST YOU!

Principle number 1: MIND

> Focus on the objective and see the result from the beginning. There is no mountain too high for you to climb.

> [10] Create in me a clean heart, O God; and renew
> a right spirit within me. Psalm 51:10 (KJV)

Principle number 2: PHYSIQUE

> Develop a "Yes, I can" attitude.

> You should know you better than anyone.

> Make the mirror your best friend. This is not to be arrogant or conceited but to examine yourself so you can see your flaws before anyone else notices them.

> [13] I can do all things through Christ who strengthens me.
> Philippians 4:13 (NKJV)

Principle number 3: DIET

> One thing to remember is this: Whatever you put into your mind or your body that is unproductive is

considered junk. Whatever food you put into your mouth must have nutritional value; otherwise, your body will reject it. Therefore, treat yourself as the temple of God.

[16] Do you not know that you are the temple of God and *that* the Spirit of God dwells in you?
1 Corinthians 3:16 (NKJV)

CHAPTER 16

Facing Inequality

High school is a place where young minds are still developing with creative ideas and future goals. It is a place where young people get a chance to challenge their subjects. I never questioned the purpose for the two cafeterias on one floor that were next to each other at Westhill High School. It was different back then than it is today. Students were separated during both lunch periods. The minority students were on one side, and the white students were on the other. Even the minority side was separated into two. If you were from Africa or anywhere in the Caribbean, there was only one section to congregate. Otherwise, you would face being teased by other minorities students. Name-calling like "rasta boy," for the Jamaican students, and "banana boat," for the Haitian students, was prevalent.

Another time I encountered racism was in nineth-grade history class—second floor, room 201, sixth period, during the month of February, which is the month that is legally recognized as Black History Month in America. Back then, however, during my time in high school, celebrating black history was unheard of. It was amazing to me; as we were studying European history, its culture, and the short stories of the Native Americans, the bulk of the stories were of settlers in the new land. It was interesting and strange that a vast amount of information was provided about these groups, particularly the Europeans and the settlers; however, the book only had two full pages that mentioned black history as if there were no contributions made by blacks to the development of the United States.

Mind you, the class was diverse, and the teacher was white. And here I was, a young man speaking with a heavy accent, challenging the author of the book, not the teacher. Well, the teacher took great offense to my inquiries, which were valid. Why were there only two pages mentioning black history in the book? Why no inclusion of how blacks arrived in America? What locations in America did the slaves get dropped off to? How were they being sold? What happened to the slaves in the plantation? What happened to the slaves in the house? Why were they called house niggers? Why were the light-skinned blacks called mulattoes? What happened with the Louisiana purchase, and why did it happen?

I guess the questions made him feel infuriated. He seemed to think, "Here is this black kid from Haiti challenging my whiteness." It was not a confrontation but more of a debate, and I believe he was ill-equipped to debate about history or even teach the subject. I felt the book provided little information to help him. This revealed to me that the system that created the curriculum was divisive. How can you teach a history class and leave out a whole portion of history? It is incomplete. His ignorance was confirmed when he said, "Young man, go meet me in the principal's office." I was suspended for "disturbing the class."

I think had the school system provided the students with basic information about history from primary school to secondary school, we would not have as many issues as we have today regarding racism. One of the elements causing this disparity is the lack of providing broad, complete information on the historical background of all cultures. If our students were taught early on, things would be different today. People of all races would have a level playing ground with no need to feel they had to fight for equal rights. The understanding provided by the education would create a sense of morality. Yes, it is good to provide a historical background of the

Europeans in America, as well as the history of the settlers, but black history has equal value.

Another time I was faced with racism was in auto mechanic shop class. As usual, I was surrounded by white students. I was probably the most creative person in the class. The name-calling never stopped, and the teacher never even flinched. Silence oftentimes means that you are in agreement. It was during tenth grade, and I was at the top of the class in terms of grades. One day the assistant principal brought his vehicle in to have the head gasket changed. This type of work goes to the intermediate mechanic class. When the project came to the shop, the best student would get the job first. There was a huge argument among my classmates where many were saying I should not get the job over them because they were white. The name-calling escalated, and I was being referenced as a "nigger."

The teacher did a draw, and I lost. I did not have any one on my team as I was considered the black sheep. The teacher monitored everything to be sure all was under control. He made it a lesson, explaining that whoever is doing a job must explain exactly what is involved and how they plan to execute it. By this time, the vehicle was on the bay, ready to be lifted off, but the job did not require for the car to be lifted until time to change the oil. The winners were so excited. I was happy they would be doing the job because I did not want my hands dirty that day.

The only universal wrench available to the entire shop, accidentally fell in the intake manifold while someone was removing the old gasket. The one-hour class turned into a two-hour class because no one could figure out how to retrieve the wrench in the winding manifold pipe, not even the teacher. Around that time, the maker of the universal wrench provided all the local high schools with mechanic shops a gift—the universal wrench). The wrench was part a promotion, introducing a good tool to do a certain difficult job.

Based on where the tool was lodged, it was almost impossible to take out. Some suggested leaving the car in the air; however, the length and the curve of the pipe made that impossible. Others suggested cutting the pipe, but that was a cost that the assistant principal did not factor into his budget. The teacher wanted to keep this a secret because it would be an embarrassment for him.

The teacher looked at me and said, "What do you suggest? Remember, this will go toward your project grade."

I told him I needed the area cleared of my classmates but that he should remain. Another argument started, along with the name-calling. I ignored the name-calling and expressed to the teacher that I wanted straight As for the rest of the year if I was able to retrieve the universal wrench from the winding pipe. He agreed, with these conditions: "If you lose, every week you come to class, you would be the one cleaning the shop and putting away all the garbage." I accepted his conditions.

My classmates swore this black kid, the banana boat boy, couldn't do it. The teacher happened to love chewing gum all the time, and I asked him to let me have it. Just imagine the name-calling at this point.

I did a sound test to hear the location of the tool. I took a tape meter, and I measured the length. I asked the teacher for a metal clothes hanger. I secured the gum at the end of the stretched hanger, and I slowly slid it into the hole. There was complete silence during this time. I know if I was not able to pull this off, that would have been it for me. As I was pulling the hanger back up, there was the universal wrench. I earned my classmates' respect, and the teacher kept his end of the deal. All of a sudden, some of the kids began questioning my blackness. One classmate said, "You're not black!" That was an insult. It was as if he was saying that a black person can't think outside of the box and come up with solutions. In addition, he made a certificate and wrote on it, "This day Pierre d'Haiti used a clothes hanger with a piece of chewed gum on it and removed a stuck universal wrench out of a manifold pipe." He posted it on top of the chalk board for future mechanics so they could learn that being an auto mechanic also involves creativity. I overcame such prejudice and racism through creativity. I encourage you as well, when in a bind, to use your imagination and find creative ways to get yourself out.

Last time I experienced racism in school was in a college drafting class. All throughout high school, I wanted to become a mechanical drafting designer. I was the only black student in the class. Mind you, since high school, I took time to study the design of engine shafts, pistons, and carburetors, among other aspects of mechanical design. In class, every time we were assigned a project, I always finished first. The teacher became annoyed and would tell me go sit down and wait; wait until a white student comes up to him with a completed project first, then he would accept mine. This happened more frequently as the projects became more difficult. I would present my final draft, and he would say, "Give me a minute." By then, I knew the routine. He even sent one of the students to me, and she literally copied my example. The professor took the white student's project instead of mine.

The students were observing how I was being treated by the professor. The one who copied my example went to him, demanding an explanation for why he was treating me like that. She was honest and told him that she copied the project line by line and word for word. She questioned why he took hers instead of mine. Both her and a couple of other students went to the dean's office to file a complaint. He was fired. I, along with a few other conscientious white students, left the school. I believe not all white folks are racists. Only God can bring the good ones your way.

CHAPTER 17

Where Did The Snow Go?

The best time of my life was during snow season in high school.

It started when we lived on Fairfield Avenue on the westside of Stamford. I always looked forward to the snow, whether during school or on winter vacation. The snow did me good. It provided for me. I bought my first car with the money I made from shoveling snow. Back in the day, when it snowed, it was a fun time. It wasn't like today; when it snows, school closes, and everyone is stuck at home. If I missed a class period in the morning at school, one of the old ladies I shoveled for would make a phone call on my behalf to let the school know exactly where I was and what time to expect me there. They were like angels to me.

Snow season in the 80s would produce two, sometimes four, feet of snow, and yet we would still go to school and go about other businesses. For me, it was my snow-removal business. I started with the houses nearby for $20 a driveway including sidewalks; after removing the snow from the seventh driveway, I was doing pretty good.

Some of the people were older folks, and they loved me. They would not let anyone else touch their driveway. In fact, they became my word-of-mouth advertising agency. At one point, I had twenty-one driveways to clean. They knew where I lived and which school

I went. They would pay a taxi to pick me up so that I can come and clean their driveway. They would make sure I had a warm cup of chocolate milk or tea. I owe these folks a debt of gratitude for they believed in me. When I was going away to college, one lady told me not to go too far so that I would be available to clean her driveway. The money was good. Some of these people loved me so much, and I believe they did not pay me just to remove the snow for them but to invest in my future because they saw something in me.

Some of my customers would give me Christmas cards with money in them. My well-being was important to them. I was not just a black kid hustling in the snow and cutting grass. I was a kid they expected to see become somebody. They made sure they brought me to the college dormitory and helped me arranged my room. Thank you, Mr. and Mrs. McNelly, for being my secondary parents.

CHAPTER 18

Shattered Dream

Frankly, I wanted to become a mechanical engineer, designing jet engines and motors. I spent a lot of time in my teenage years in high school studying the makeup of mechanical equipment and motor parts. I became good at it. I spent a lot of time in the school drafting room, testing my designs. My brothers and I were always comparing thoughts and ideas about mechanical parts, especially their makeup and purpose. I wanted to go to Michigan to work for the Ford Motor Company, but God had other plans.

During my last year in high school, I took a small chain motor from a WEEDWACKER. I hooked it on the wheel of a wooden skateboard and screwed it to the back. I used it as my twelfth grade project. It allowed for riding on a slow-moving motorized skateboard. That thing could only go two miles per hour, but it was so much fun!

That dream was squashed by the experiences of prejudice I encountered in college.

Your dream may be shattered, but ask the master what his plan is for you. He will direct your path.

CHAPTER 19

You Need Help!

You see the garden operates in seasons; each season brings its own experiences. There is a season where everything seems dead and cold; that is the winter season.

In the following season, that which was dead and frozen begin to show buds and flowers as it is fed with sun and rain; that is the spring season.

Yet another season appears, where buds and flowers are in full bloom among the brightest green; and we call it summer.

Finally, after that which was dead and frozen in winter becomes green in spring, providing shade in summer and allowing the ground to receive seed for planting, change begins and allows for harvesting; we call this autumn.

This cycle goes around and around, repeating itself. The seasons themselves never alter, but we change because of our behavior and attitude.

Life is similar to the garden in the seasons. Sometimes circumstances and situations can cause us to be out of focus because of no fault of our own. Remaining in the garden of life dry and in the same position for a long time is a signal that you need help. You may remember situations in your life years back and hang on to the thoughts of "it used to be," "I wish I did, "or "I could have been."

Now is the time to dust yourself off and move on. We sometimes allow resentment and bitterness to take control of our relationship with other people. The emotions we experience can be a result of keeping old baggage in the cabinet of our soul, and holding on to it can delay future progress.

CHAPTER 20

Paradigm Shift

Many people, even those in my circle of friends, did not know where I found my enjoyment, happiness, or comfort. Hiding who I really was and what I was feeling began after I had the bad experiences of prejudice in college. I entered another local college, the Norwalk Technical Community College, in hopes that I would find my passion again.

A paradigm shift happens when your sense of reality changes. Views on how the world works—what is possible, important, valuable, safe, or acceptable—begin to shift. I created my first paradigm shift through my change of major in college. It was a way to clear out some shame that was causing discouragement. I found a job in the field of human services that changed my direction. I was working for the Department of Developmental Services, formerly the DMR, at a time when the Mansfield Training School was on its way to closure and Southbury Training school was still in the process of closing.

The Mansfield Training School and Hospital was a state-run facility for the mentally retarded located in Mansfield, Connecticut. It was active from 1860 to 1993.

The hospital opened in Lakeville in 1860 as the Connecticut School for Imbeciles at Lakeville. Its name was changed to the Connecticut Training School for the Feebleminded at Lakeville in 1915. Two years later, it merged with the Connecticut Colony for Epileptics (founded at Mansfield in 1910) and acquired its present name.

When it opened in 1917, the merged institution had 402 students in residence. By 1932, the resident population had grown to 1,070. During the Depression and World War II, demand for its services increased, resulting in both overcrowding and long waiting lists for new enrollments. Staffing levels increased during the 1960s as philosophies on treatment of mental retardation changed, and there were 1,609 residents and 875 full-time staff as of 1969. During the 1970s and 1980s, many residents were relocated from dormitories to on-campus cottages or to group homes located around the state. By 1976, the resident population had dropped to 1,106, and by 1991 just 141 people remained as residents.
https://en.wikipedia.org/wiki/Mansfield_Training_School_and_Hospital

The switch from dormitories to on-campus cottages became the way to deinstitutionalize the system, whereby creating a way to integrate the mental retardation population into their local community. There are many of these "centers," as we call them, throughout the state. I started in the west region Lower Fairfield Center (LFC) campus; however, I have had the opportunity to work in many different centers throughout the state. I met some of the most wonderful staff who really enjoy the human services field. These people had heart; after all, that is what it takes to work in this field; it is a job that is certainly not for everyone.

The story I am about to share with you is important to me. Just as I was left in the garden at a young age, so it was with those I worked with who had developmental disabilities and mental issues. They were left in the garden of the system, if you will. These people have real names, but I prefer to use different names to tell the story.

Not all mental retardation or intellectual disability is the same. Each case poses different challenges and, therefore, must be treated differently. You must find what works for each individual case and stick to it.

Since I created the paradigm shift, I brought myself close to the high truth concerning my value and purpose in life. I went from beliefs that were keeping me at a distance from the amazing life experiences written in my soul to those that helped me shine.

Tiny was a tall Caucasian man who was nonverbal. He expressed his wants and needs by saying, "bubububububu." He was a very nice guy, but if he did not get what he desired, he would slap his head, and if staff was nearby, they'd receive a hit as well.

Sista was a Caucasian female who verbalized her wants and needs rather loudly. She was a nice lady but could be very demanding; if she did not get what she wanted, she would force her way to get it.

Buddy was a short African American male who was nonverbal. He expressed his wants and needs by using basic sign language. He slapped his head nonstop when he was frustrated. That could go on for hours and hours. No one could figure out why he was doing this because he was not able to communicate his problem. Buddy and I became friends. I know he accepted me as such when he welcomed me by holding my hands. He would come to me as if I was the center of his world. He was a very loving guy. When he was walking from home to the day program, which was across the way from his cottage, you could literally hear his feet dragging because he had one leg longer than the other. If he was not in a good mood, you could hear him across the way, slapping his head. So at the Adult Day Program (ADP), we knew, if Buddy was not in good spirits, there was a good chance it was not going to be a good day for us.

This type of behavior from Buddy could go on for weeks. We had tried many different strategies to assist him during his time of frustration. Buddy and I would go on adventures, doing anything to keep his hands busy so that he would not slap his head. Psychologists have described this as self-injurious behavior (SIB). We all have exhibited SIB in one way or another, such as constant lip-biting or fingernail-biting. Some say the cause is anxiety or nervousness. It takes a lot of compassion and patience to work in this field.

Unfortunately, Buddy passed away in a cold, freezing winter season. I felt that Buddy had left me in the garden just when our relationship began to flourish. I did not have a chance to say goodbye.

Pipo was a Caucasian male who was very friendly. He loved to be around people and enjoyed having the same conversation over and over. He was a hard worker who liked his routine activities to remain the same. He would take his medication, but before he took it, he would play around and say, "Nasty medicine, yuk, nasty little medicine."

These folks were the most fun people to be with.

This was a time when mechanical restraint was acceptable, though it did seem cruel. For some of the individuals and the issues they had, this method was required, and it helped relieve frustration. Autism, back then, was barely a word in our vocabulary. It was difficult to understand the person who suffered from it as it did not have a name.

I worked at the ADP as a state school instructor. I found this department interesting because we were part of the solution to individual development. It was sad because after a period of working with an individual, as soon as there were signs of progress, the team would decide at the annual meeting that it was time for the individual to move on to the next chapter of life. A strong bond had been forged with students, and it was hard to see them go. I always looked forward to going to work because I knew there would always be some kind of fun.

One day we went to a TJ Maxx store in Norwalk, and I asked for any leftover clothing or material they may be able to donate. My guys were willing to turn this into a small project, so the manager said yes, they would make a donation. I received the approval from my organization's management to accept it. As a result, my students and other students participated in a community service program, whereby their presence became visible and accepted. We created a store at ADP with the donated items and gave them out free of charge. The store was run by Buddy, Sista, Tiny, and Speedy, and they were servicing the two centers within the West Region LFC and EGC. It was even open to those living in the group home.

As a result of this incidental teaching, we saw a huge decrease in negative behaviors and an increase in a sense of accomplishment, pride, acceptance, and happiness.

Yet another interesting and creative idea came about when the store began to grow. More staff was needed to run it, five days a week, because we were dealing with folks whose attention span was very short. I liked to think of active ways to improve the lives of those under my care and have them participate in the endeavors. We gathered boxes and created a robot that literally talked; we recorded the voices of the staff. Pushing the buttons and hearing their voices caused them to redirect any unruly or undesirable behavior. It was a means of redirecting them to the task at hand. Our creation had become the hottest item of the entire program. I was very proud of these guys.

After the death of Buddy, I acquired a distaste for the field. I left the industry and went into politics and banking. It had been about ten years later. I was coming from a training for a bank in New Jersey. I dropped by in Greenwich, Connecticut, to one of the supermarkets, to grab a sandwich. As I was going through the aisle, searching for a bag of potato chips to go with my tuna fish sandwich, I heard a deep voice calling me. "Hello, Pierre."

I turned around, and there was Pipo. We engaged in a nice conversation, where he was recalling our experiences together. His job coach had no idea who I was and had no notion of our conversation. All she noticed was this tall intellectual disabled man in the store having a conversation with another man.

Pipo said, "This Pierre was my instructor." He proceeded, "Do you want to work with me?"

I said, "I don't know." I gave him my card so that he would have something from me. So he went straight to the agency office, looking for the manager, and told him he wanted Pierre to work with him.

Three days later, I got a phone call from the agency, demanding that I come to work with Pipo because my name would not come off his lips. So I accepted and left the bank, going back to work with the population I loved so much.

CHAPTER 21

The Code

Directory Code: 104210
Publisher Code: 0791

The definition of a code is a set of rules or a system of communication, often with randomly assigned numbers and letters given specific meanings.

Yellow Pages refer to a telephone directory of businesses, organized by category, rather than alphabetically, by business name and in which advertising is sold. The directories were originally printed on yellow paper as opposed to white pages for noncommercial listings. The traditional term "yellow pages" are now also applied to online directories of businesses. In many countries, including Canada, the United Kingdom, Australia, and elsewhere, *Yellow Pages*, as well as the "walking fingers" logo first introduced in the 1970s by the Bell System-era AT&T, are registered trademarks, though the owner varies from country to country, usually being held by the main national telephone company. https://www.google.com/search?client=firefox-b-1-d&sxsrf=ALeKk027eYYDRY okGrFpaT2Dq2xXzgNVA:1592533083880&q=code+definition&spell=1&sa=X&ved=2ahUKEwiGvYeG6IzqAhXtlXIEHdHqDX0QirwEKAB6BAgWECc&biw=1366&bih=654

In order for any publisher to have access to the national, regional, state, towns, and cities telephone data with addresses, they must have the CODE, and this code system is provided by the telephone giants because they have direct access to individual addresses and telephone numbers.

There were no African Americans in the Yellow Pages or directory business. As such, it was a challenge getting in the industry because it was controlled by the giants. Unfortunately, the African American community was categorized as part of the general population in the industry; nonetheless, visibility appeared to be low. It was very difficult for any business targeting the African American community to directly penetrate, unless going through the census tracks, and these phone companies had all the information. What is that information? It's all the addresses and phone numbers. Every address and phone number were generalized, and therefore, to recognize African Americans in the yellow pages was a daunting task.

Looking at the population density through the lens of the census bureau, we were able to identify African Americans within a certain census track, which meant we had to go track by track and block by block to figure this out. The numbers would not include the African Americans who were living outside of the identified tracks. Going back to the Yellow Pages strategy, we found that there were no inclusive plans for African Americans. As a result, we created a directory targeting the African American community directly.

During the process of our third directory, a letter came, stating that "we recognize you under our radar, please contact us." I immediately contacted our lawyer who got in touch with the person who sent the letter. Mind you, we had sent in our application request for access to the yellow pages code, and it was denied. They requested a meeting, and my lawyer suggested we have a preliminary conversation, and we did. It did not go very well. Meanwhile, we were getting ready for production of the third directory. I clearly saw that these giants had no intention of including us or giving us access to the code. My lawyer told me I should leave it alone because a lot of money would be required to further the case. I went to pray and call on God, and I told him that since we had come this far, I didn't want to go back, but it was up to him.

Three weeks had gone by, and a letter came in, stating, "Mr. Pierre d'Haiti, the Association of Directory Publishers committee met, and we have approved your application for directory codes." This committee included the major phone companies and directory publishing. This meant we were now a full directory and *Yellow Pages* publisher with a certain ethnic demographic, African and Caribbean American Yellow Pages, with access to all data pertaining to directory and *Yellow Pages* publishing. Victory!

CHAPTER 22

Companion

While in college, I adopted a dog I found in the local dog pound. It was a mixed breed—German Shepherd and Rottweiler. I named him Guno. He was a faithful and protective dog, as well as a great companion to me and my parents. He watched over the house and the neighborhood. He was the best watch dog. At times it seemed like he did not sleep at night because he barked at anything and everything that moved in the neighborhood past midnight. We became best of friends. I loved just driving around with him. Guno was also a good listener. He was calm-mannered, attentive, and friendly. When I was under a lot of stress, I would sit with him and talk; he actually listened, watching me closely, fully attentive. A silent listener is sometimes the best listener. When it came to eating breakfast, lunch, and dinner, it was like he had an alarm clock that reminded him it was time to eat. My grandmother, my mother, and my stepfather all had to be around at the same time in order for him to start eating. He was so used to eating Haitian food that he would not eat any other food. Every holiday he got a huge bone, which he collected and saved underground, and he'd make sure the area where he buried the bone was well protected.

Guno died at an old age, and we all missed him terribly.

CHAPTER 23

In Full Bloom

My journey from brokenness to healing began when I was literally left in the garden as a young child. This was the day my mother was informed that we lost my father to murder. Given no answers at the time and my feelings not given importance, I felt abandoned, neglected, lonely, and deprived. That led me to seek attention and validation through destructive means.

I was metaphorically stuck in the garden, in the winter season, where everything was dead and frozen; I was not producing good fruit. It wasn't until I had an encounter with God and the power of the Holy Spirit that I began to realize the necessity of forgiveness and the release of anger, resentment, and bitterness. It was when I recognized my inability to save and heal myself that I allowed God in that garden with me.

God and I worked the ground together, allowing each season its purpose. It was then that I became free from all the mess that held me captive; it was then that I was able to recognize my God-given purposes; it was then that I was able to see my garden in full bloom.

WHAT THEY ARE SAYING ABOUT PIERRE

I recall as a young adult, Pierre organized a bus ride to Brooklyn, New York, where he brought two hundred people from Connecticut to demonstrate in a walk on the Brooklyn Bridge. This was a daunting effort where he challenged the Yellow Pages giants, The Yellow Book and Southern New England Telephone (SNET) Yellow Pages, for equality of rights—demanding African Americans obtain access for participation in the Yellow Pages industry. As a result, he was awarded the Yellow Pages code.

After the 2010 earthquake that devasted Pierre's homeland, the mayor of the city of Bridgeport assigned a project of coordinating an office to be responsible for Haiti relief efforts. Pierre jumped into action and took the challenge head on, resulting in another extraordinarily successful venture. My own city of Stamford, Connecticut, organized a project, which Pierre played a role in, where we donated medical equipment to a city in Haiti. Once again, he has proven ability in handling monumental tasks and meeting or exceeding all requirements.

He is and has always been a visionary who is talented and creative. Pierre designed the Adopt-a-City Program, which resulted in many cities from Connecticut following suit in providing some aid to a

Haitian city. Pierre's clear and unconditional love for God over the years has made it no surprise to see his service to God's people.

Should you have any questions or would like to speak with me, feel free to contact my office.

Yours truly,
Jean D. Williams
Chief Executive Officer
PLANET ECO

WHAT THEY ARE SAYING ABOUT PIERRE (CONT'D)

After the terrible earthquake in Haiti in 2010, Reverend d'Haiti formed a group of men and women to help meet the needs of the Haitian people. He did this originally under the auspices of the Mayor's Office of the city of Bridgeport. He entitled this organization Haiti Works!

Pierre recruited and empowered several men and women to make a difference. They took action and have continued to strive to fulfill Christ's command that we "Heal the sick, raise the dead" (Mathew 10:8).

Reverend d'Haiti has inspired the Haiti Works! membership to act. Last year, for example, he shared his vision that a firetruck be sent to Haiti to deal with emergency and fire response needs, and in April 2011, the firetruck, named Hope, was shipped to Petion-Ville, courtesy of the United States Air Force. How is that for inspired action!

Now Pierre has made connections with (1) Amb. Pamela White; (2) Gen. John Kelly, a four-star Marine Corps general and the commander of US Southern Command, one of the five major US Commands throughout the world; (3) US State Department; (4) US Department of Defense; and (5) US Senator Christopher Murphy to establish an emergency responder academy in Haiti.

Are you eager to know a man who lives the message of our Lord? Look no further.

Thank you for allowing me the honor of sharing who Pierre is in my own world and my life.

Yours sincerely,
Carl E. Rhode
US Army Chaplain, Retired

A LITTLE BIT ABOUT PIERRE

Publisher –   *African American Yellow Pages*
Publisher –   *Caribbean American Yellow Book*
Publisher–   *APEHC Newsletter*
Coauthor –   *Haiti/Smile and Life*
Licensed Minister,   Faith Community Church
Ordained Pastor–
Founder –   Haiti Works Incorporated
Commissioner –   Planning and Zoning Commission (P&Z)
Cofounder –   Young Haitian Association
Cofounder –   Haitian Heritage Awareness Month CT
Cofounder –   Kombit Ayisyen Pou Avansman Ak Byenet
                       (KAPAB)
Board Member –   Democracy Works Inc.
Board Member –   Greater Bridgeport Regional Planning Agency
Board Member –   In-Land Wet Land Water Courses Agency
Board member –   International Institute of Connecticut Inc.
Board member –   Southern Connecticut Regional Sickle Cell
                       Association
Board member –   Ecole Heritage Chretienne de Clisan
Executive Board   Association des Pasteurs Evangeliques
member –   Haitiens de CT. (APEHC)
Member –   Greater Bridgeport Church and Synagogues

Member –	Southern England Connecticut District Church of God
Member –	New England Baptist Convention
Member –	Shepherd Connection
Member –	Bridgeport Regional Business Council (BRBC)
Member –	West Indian American Association of Greater Bridgeport, Inc. (WIAAGB)
Member –	National Association for the Advancement of Colored People (NAACP)
Member –	Association of Directory Publishers (ADP)
Member –	Haitian American Professional Association of CT (HAPAC)
Member –	Connecticut Minority Suppliers Development Council (CMSDC)
Candidate –	Doctor of Ministries

ACKNOWLEDGMENTS

I am not qualified to write, much less pen a book, but I feel it important to recognize some people who have contributed to my life experience and, thus, in some way, to this book: Gelise Boussiquot (Mante Lise), RIP. To Marie Jose Midi, RIP. Thank you for being an example of determination. To the members of Faith Community Church of God. Sr. Nicole Nelson, you epitomize patience. Sr. Rosita Etienne, trust is what you exemplify. Christine Lamour Valeris, Sr. Yvette Tatas Pierre, through all that you endured, you put God first, and it typifies that you are a woman of Faith, "tout bagay deja byen." To Marie and Bishop William Wiggins and the Bethel Memorial Deliverance Church family, you were always there for me. Maitre Levi Nelson, of Institution Mix St. Joseph, de Petion-Ville. The Sterling Men, Chris Valante, Paul Hirsh, Carl Rohde, Wes Murphy, Carrie Legagneur (Youyou). Vaillant Domingue, Pierre Richard Paulemond, Tonya Fountain, Veronica Aiery Wilson, Rev. Mark Smith, Rev. Dr. Marcus McKinney, Rev. Joseph Michel, Rev. Jowel Papin, Dr. Fred McKinney, Angelucci Manigat, Maude Joseph, Dr. William Bertier, Gwen Edwards, Miles Rapport, Dr. Boise Kimber, Bill Finch, Paul Timpanelli, Deborah Caviness, Randy Salomon, Dr. Joyce Hamilton, Carolyn Vermont, Joe Ganim, Bishop Jean Rhau, Bishop Kenneth Hill, Michael d'Haiti, thank you for not tolerating my nonsense. It helped me stay focused. Ralph, your interrogation opens my eyes to a lot of things. And, Martine, we call you "Ma," not short for Martine, but for the motherly figure you represent.

Irene Silencieux Loiseau, Clivia Lauture, you were a great support to us after my father's death. Nicolas Jean Guillaume (Papi), you taught me friendship. Onide Jean Guillaume, RIP, thank you for your kindness. Rosemond Alix, you did a good job exemplifying what a father is by constantly reminding me that I was going to be great. I kept your promise. Thank you for teaching me about the Haitian culture and its folklore. Mario Lauture (too chill), you always pushed me to be the best. Tally Merisca, Elie Jean Guillaume, as usual you wonder where I am. "What are your up to?" Checking up on me is the norm with you. Hey, what can I say? That's what friends are for! Pierre Paulemon, Ptr. Raul Noel, during the most embarrassing time in my life, in a moment of rejection, you were there to provide words of comfort. Bro. Isidor Wilson, whether in the middle of the night or on Sunday morning on the 5:00 a.m. prayer line, should I have a revelation, you were always there to provide some type of guidance. Rev. Joseph Lalane, Fr. Frantz Deruisseaux, Evangelist Eutrope Samson, Bp. Jean Russell Bataille, Rev. Alexis Leonce, Rev. David Miler. Team KAPAB Charles Tisdale, RIP; Joan Gibson; Miles Rappaport; Atty. Philip Berns; Atty. John Lacava; Ronnie Delva; Fanel Melville; James St. Paul; Serge Bourssiquot; Emanuel Doreste; Elza Jolicoeur; Molver Fiefe; Pierre Clovitch. Team Haiti Works Inc.; Atty. Charles Willinger; Peter diNatale; James Kavalines; Patricia Gallegos; Mitch Edwards; Eriks Sumanis; Lee Rosen; Sam Wilson, CPA; Michelle Lyons. Team Haitian Heritage Awareness Month of CT Dionne Lamothe, Pascale Milien, Claudy Jacques, Jean Rene, Kislene, Pierre Deruisseaux, Marie Yves, Mitch Noel, Guy Bocicaut, Lydia Martinez, Rosa Corea, Charles Forbin, Claudomiro Falcon, Ernie Lauture, Jacques Rene, Marie Laura Caserta, Mr. and Mrs. McNelly, and finally, Dr. R. A. Vernon, thank you for spiritual insight and for encouragement to THINK BIG.

35 The desert and the parched land will be glad; the wilderness will rejoice and blossom.

Like the crocus, ² it will burst into bloom; it will rejoice greatly and shout for joy. The glory of Lebanon will be given to it, the splendor of Carmel and Sharon; they will see the glory of the LORD, the splendor of our God. ³ Strengthen the feeble hands, steady the knees that give way; ⁴ say to those with fearful hearts, "Be strong, do not fear; your God will come, he will come with vengeance; with divine retribution he will come to save you." ⁵ Then will the eyes of the blind be opened and the ears of the deaf unstopped. ⁶ Then will the lame leap like a deer, and the mute tongue shout for joy. Water will gush forth in the wilderness and streams in the desert. ⁷ The burning sand will become a pool, the thirsty ground bubbling springs. In the haunts where jackals once lay, grass and reeds and papyrus will grow. ⁸ And a highway will be there; it will be called the Way of Holiness; it will be for those who walk on that Way. The unclean will not journey on it; wicked fools will not go about on it. ⁹ No lion will be there, nor any ravenous beast; they will not be found there. But only the redeemed will walk there, ¹⁰ and those the LORD has rescued will return. They will enter Zion with singing; everlasting joy will crown their heads. Gladness and joy will overtake them, and sorrow and sighing will flee away.

START JOURNALING YOUR LIFE

WHAT DO YOU MISS?

_____

_____

_____

_____

_____

_____

_____

_____

_____

_____

_____

_____

_____

_____

_____

_____

_____

_____

_____

_____

_____

_____

_____

_____

_____

WHAT DID YOU LEARNED ABOUT THE PEOPLE YOU TRUST?

WHAT IS YOUR FAVORITE MEMORY OF YOUR FATHER?

WHAT DID YOU LIKE, AND WHAT WERE YOU GOOD AT?

_____

_____

_____

_____

_____

_____

_____

_____

_____

_____

_____

_____

_____

_____

_____

_____

_____

_____

_____

_____

_____

_____

_____

DID YOU EVER REBEL? WHAT DID YOU DO?

_____

_____

_____

_____

_____

_____

_____

_____

_____

_____

_____

_____

_____

_____

_____

_____

_____

_____

_____

_____

_____

_____

_____

WHAT WAS IT LIKE GROWING UP?